Practicing Conscious Living and Dying

Stories of the Eternal Continuum of Consciousness

First published by O Books, 2008
O Books is an imprint of John Hunt Publishing
Ltd., The Bothy, Deershot Lodge, Park Lane,
Ropley, Hants, SO24 0BE, UK
office1@o-books.net
www.o-books.net

Distribution in:

UK and Europe
Orca Book Services
orders@orcabookservices.co.uk
Tel: 01202 665432 Fax: 01202 666219 Int. code
(44)

USA and Canada
NBN
custserv@nbnbooks.com
Tel: 1 800 462 6420 Fax: 1 800 338 4550

Australia and New Zealand
Brumby Books
sales@brumbybooks.com.au
Tel: 61 3 9761 5535 Fax: 61 3 9761 7095

Far East (offices in Singapore, Thailand, Hong
Kong, Taiwan)
Pansing Distribution Pte Ltd
kemal@pansing.com
Tel: 65 6319 9939 Fax: 65 6462 5761

South Africa
Alternative Books
altbook@peterhyde.co.za
Tel: 021 555 4027 Fax: 021 447 1430

Text copyright Annamaria Hemingway 2008

Design: Stuart Davies

ISBN: 978 1 84694 077 4

Printed in the US by Maple Vail

O Books operates a distinctive and ethical publishing philosophy in
all areas of its business, from its global network of authors to
production and worldwide distribution.

No trees were cut down to print this particular book. The paper is
100% recycled, with 50% of that being post-consumer. It's processed
chlorine-free, and has no fibre from ancient or endangered forests.

This production method on this print run saved approximately
thirteen trees, 4,000 gallons of water, 600 pounds of solid waste,
990 pounds of greenhouse gases and 8 million BTU of energy. On its
publication a tree was planted in a new forest that O Books is
sponsoring at The Village www.thefourgates.com

Practicing Conscious Living and Dying

Stories of the Eternal Continuum of Consciousness

Annamaria Hemingway

BOOKS

Winchester, UK
Washington, USA

True wisdom comes to each of us when we realize how little we understand about life, ourselves, and the world around us.
Socrates

For Vanna, a woman full of grace, and my darling buds of May, Jay and Toby

CONTENTS

ACKNOWLEDGMENTS

I would like to thank the following people for their contributions, encouragement and support in the writing of this book:

Tiffany Snow, Dave Bennet, Richie Arrellano, Larry Hagman, Joanne Cacciatore, Peter Samuelson, Wilma Melville, Sally and Donald Goodrich, Andy Lakey, Keith and Francesca Richardson, Suzanne De Wees, Carol Brown, Sandra Cook, and John and Mary-Ellen McGee.

I would also like to acknowledge and extend a special thank you to: Jonathan Collins, for helping me to make one of my dreams a reality and contributing to some of the early stories; Richard Palmer, for gathering wood to rekindle my fire; Gael Beldon, for her constant friendship and our philosophical walks with our treasured companions, Jack and Epiphany, that always provided me with a source of inspiration; Reuben Beckham, for his continuous support and always reminding me of the spiritual dimension of life; Karen Hall, for all her technical assistance; Emily Collins, for her help in promoting and publicizing this book.

A special thank you to John Griffin, for contributing to the text material, introducing three of the stories, and his collaboration in the writing of Larry's Story and Richie's Story.

Finally, I would like to thank all those in spirit who continue to inspire, protect, and guide me. Their physical presence may no longer be seen, but their voices are still clearly heard.

NEAR-DEATH EXPERIENCES - NOT THE END, BUT A NEW BEGINNING

I have good hope that there is something remaining for the dead
Socrates

Recently, near-death experience (NDE) has entered the sphere of public awareness and been the subject of much scientific scrutiny and philosophical discussion. In 1982, George Gallup, Jr. published *Adventures in Immortality*, a book detailing the results of his own survey into the phenomenon. Among his discoveries: fifteen percent of those interviewed had experienced a close brush with death, and thirty-four percent of those reported an accompanying out-of-body experience, which included a peaceful feeling as they felt themselves entering another realm of existence. Many of these individuals also described a rapid life review, during which their entire lives flashed through consciousness.

Comparable surveys carried out in Europe and India have produced similar findings. The true figures regarding NDEs are likely far higher, as many people are reluctant to disclose such experiences in a world that is often hostile to the validity of the near-death experience. Nevertheless, instances of such temporary visits to an afterlife by persons who have been determined clinically dead — and then "come back to life"— have been recorded throughout human history.

In France and Spain, depictions of otherworldly journeys have been recorded in the form of murals dating from the Upper Paleolithic civilizations, preserving ancient visionary accounts of transcendence over death. Early written testimonies of the near-death experience include an eighth-century account from Venerable Bede's *A History of the English Church and People*, in which he relates the story of a man who had died, but was later found to be alive (much to the surprise of his distraught relatives). The man sat up and described his encounter with a figure in a white robe, who took him to a beautiful meadow where a luminous light was shining. The revived man was reluctant to return to his physical body, but upon doing so, decided to live the rest of his life very differently: relinquishing all of his worldly goods and responsibilities, he became a monk.

A more contemporary and widely known NDE account is that of Black Elk, a revered medicine man of the Oglala Sioux tribe. As a young boy in the late nineteenth century, he suffered a serious illness and appeared to be dying. Upon losing consciousness, his spirit left his physical body. He crossed the threshold into the spirit world, where he experienced a "Great Vision" and realized that he was in the presence of the Powers of the World. Black Elk was told that he must return to his physical body, newly endowed with special powers and a mission to fulfill. That he should receive this vision at a time when his entire people and culture were facing annihilation from the "white man" is not an uncommon occurence. Similar apocalyptic visions have often been experienced during crucial periods in world history.

Over the centuries, numerous other accounts of NDE have been recorded in different cultures and countries throughout the world. NDEs occur in children as well as adults, though childhood NDEs in general seem simpler and less intense than those related by adults.

Studies reveal that religious orientation is not a necessary prerequisite to having an NDE; some of those who have undergone NDEs had no prior belief in any concept of God, and described themselves as agnostics. Interestingly, it has also been determined that belief in a higher power — along with a change in personal values — seems to be an invariable outcome of NDEs experienced by those with no prior religious convictions.

The mystery of the meaning of existence has been pondered by all the great philosophers. According to Greek tradition, the disciples of Plato implored their dying teacher to give them guidance on how to continue in their quest for the realization of the true meaning of philosophy as the literal love of wisdom and the wisdom of love. "Practice Dying," was his reply. The English word *practice* hasn't changed much from its original Greek source *prakike*, which means to do the work necessary to make something useful happen.

For many people, Plato's final words are hard to translate into a meaningful context, for certainly in Western societies dying is considered to be a process that results in cessation of life for the physical body. But contrary to widely-held beliefs that view the brain as the source of consciousness, there is much research to indicate that consciousness survives the body-brain demise. This was certainly the belief of Plato and Socrates.

Plato considered recounting a near-death experience to be the perfect ending for his famous Socratic dialogue. The *Republic* illustrates the rewards, for the individual and society, of living a life dedicated to justice and concern for others. This account provides a Platonic-Socratic model for the practice of dying as a means of understanding the best way to live one's life.

The story Plato tells is referred to as a myth, from the Greek *mythos*. These poetic, mythological stories bridge the gap between the profane and sacred aspects of life, through analogy. The teachings contained in their symbolic, archetypal images serve to reconnect the individual with long-forgotten and ancient truths. They embody the wisdom of an expanded form of consciousness, through which we can glimpse the ultimate destiny of the soul.

Myth also serves to unite us with the natural world, where there are constant symbolic reminders of the cycles of birth, death and rebirth. Nature provides the human being with an image of wholeness that can be accessed through observing this constant process of death and renewal, which is the ultimate truth of existence. However, this connection to our Divine heritage is often lost, and anything to do with the subject of death and dying is shunned. Why would we practice dying, when we are living life? What do the words of Plato mean today?

In the world of ancient Greece, religion was viewed as part of culture and reality. The Gods made their presence felt in society, and were believed to be masters of divination. The Greeks oriented their lives in accordance with the wishes of their deities, and would consult oracles for advice, whereupon a Priest or Priestess would channel messages from the divinities. The Greeks believed that if they lived a moral life which fulfilled the requirements of the Gods, they would be rewarded for their efforts, both in this world and the afterlife.

Plato presented *The Myth of Er,* to illustrate that the art of dying well was the culmination of living well. In this story, the hero is identified by his own name and the name of his father (Armenius) as well. The hero's city-state (Pamphylia) is also given. This may indicate that Plato is drawing upon an actual account of Er, the warrior, the son of Armenius of Pamphylia. Either way, it is certainly philosophically and psychologically true.

In this tale, the valiant Greek soldier Er is supposedly killed in combat. But when the dead are taken for burial ten days later, Er's body shows no signs of decay, even though it displays no detectable vital signs. Much to the astonishment of his comrades, Er comes back to life. Though he didn't know how he had returned to his physical body, he woke up to find himself lying on the funeral pyre at dawn. Consequently, he told of a temporary visit to the afterlife.

According to Er's account, when his soul left his body, he found himself with many other souls on a "journey" which led him to a "marvelous place," and he saw two openings side by side in the earth, and two in the sky above. In between sat judges who determined the fates of the just and the unjust. The former were given "tokens," and then they were instructed to, "take the way to the right upwards through the sky." The unjust were advised of their misdeeds, and then were "commanded to take the downward road to the left." When Er appeared before the judges, they informed him that he was to observe and learn, and then return to earthly life and describe what he had seen.

Er then viewed the souls of the just coming into a meadow from one of the openings in the sky, and the unjust filing in from one of the openings in the earth. While resting, they recounted their stories of suffering, or of enjoyment and bliss. After seven days in the meadow, on the eighth day, they all moved on to the Spindle of Necessity, through which the life cycles of the cosmos revolve. This symbolic spindle turned on Necessity's knees, and her three daughters helped to keep it in motion. One of the daughters, Lachesis, supplied the number of lots and sample lives which the souls could choose from, and they were told:

> The word of Lachesis, maiden daughter of Necessity. Souls of a day, here shall begin a new round of earthly life, to end in death. No guardian spirit will cast lots for you, but you shall choose your own destiny. Let him to who the first lot falls choose first a life to which he will be bound of necessity. But virtue owns no master: as a man honors or dishonors her, so he shall have more of her or less. The blame is his who chooses; Heaven is blameless.

Now the souls, including Er, were ready to be sent into the world again. The Interpreter scattered lots amongst them, and the souls gathered them up. Then they selected their next lives on earth. Many of the souls, though they had undergone suffering for their previous sins, remained ignorant in many fundamental ways. They still made wrong choices, which would lead them into new sins and further punishment. Souls who had come from Heaven and were not "disciplined by suffering," also chose foolishly.

Other famous figures from Greek history were also present, and were choosing their own future lives. Odysseus opted for one of quiet obscurity, as a contrast to his previous hyper-adventurous earthly existence. The soul of Ajax, a Greek hero from the siege of Troy, selected the form of a lion, as he was still bitter about the lot of men. Agamemnon — leader of the Greeks during the Trojan War and later murdered by his wife, Clytemnestra – decided on the life of an eagle. Orpheus, the Greek poet and musician who had the ability to tame even the most ferocious beasts with his beautiful melodies, picked the life of a swan.

Looking at the myth of Er from the perspective of contemporary NDEs, it symbolizes and illustrates the ability of consciousness to function independently of the body, which is a state also described in the ecstatic otherworldly journeys of the shamans whose transcendent powers were recognized and valued in many indigenous cultures. Ancient myths originating in the Orient told of similar ascensions to heavenly realms. As Eliade states in *Shamanism: Archaic Techniques of Ecstasy:*

> Er sees, among other things, the colors of heaven and the central axis, as well as the fates of men decreed by the stars. This ecstatic vision of astrological destiny can be compared with the myths, of Oriental origin, concerning The Tree of Life or the "heavenly book," on the leaves of pages of which the fates of men were inscribed. The symbolism of a "celestial book" containing fate and communicated by God to sovereigns and prophets, after their ascent to heaven, is very ancient and widely disseminated in the Orient.

It is through a similar ecstatic journey of ascension into an altered state of consciousness that Er gains insight and revelations into the workings of the cosmos. Eliade comments further:

> It is by an ecstatic vision that he is brought to understand the mystery of destiny and of existence after death…nothing changes in this gaining consciousness of ultimate reality; it is through ecstasy that man fully realizes his situation in the world and his final destiny.

Altered states of awareness, as described in the NDE, were once voiced only by poets, philosophers and mystics endowed with the ability to transcend everyday consciousness. These individuals expanded their creative imaginations to go beyond the limitations of human understanding, glimpsing the destination of the soul's journey. In the poetic masterpiece *The Divine Comedy*, Dante seeks to convey the life of the soul after death in accordance with the beliefs of medieval Christians, whereby choices in life determined the soul's fate. He describes his descent into the underworld, and the trials he encounters wandering through the realms of hell and purgatory. Dante emerges having undergone an initiation and purification, and his ascent into the celestial realms, where he is reunited with the brilliant light and truth of a divine source, features many aspects associated with NDEs. These include: witnessing the miracle of creation, viewing the entire cosmos, hearing the most magnificent music, and finding himself forever changed by the experience.

Dante's medieval visionary work is rich in spiritual symbolism, and is widely believed to have been influenced by the experience of the prophet Muhammad, who reportedly underwent a mystical nocturnal journey known as the *Mir'aj*. Although it is stated that Muhammad's physical body never left his bed that night, it is very possible that he had an out-of-body experience, which enabled his spiritual essence to ascend through the seven heavens and into the presence of God, where he was given many insights into the ultimate truth of the mystery of creation.

Modern day resuscitation techniques have prompted a great deal of scientific research and discussion of NDE. There are many individuals who deny the reality of the afterlife which this phenomenon represents. Skeptics who are scientifically inclined contend that this type of experience is probably a chemically-derived or induced hallucination of the dying brain. But there is much evidence to dispute this contention, much of it from leading experts in the field. They contend that advances in quantum electrodynamics prove that it is impossible for the brain to generate consciousness — which implies the existence of a non-biological aspect of the human being, more commonly referred to as the soul.

In 2001, *The Lancet* (an international medical journal) published the findings of scientific studies carried out in ten different Dutch hospitals over a period of thirteen years. The studies involved interviews with people who were resuscitated after being declared clinically dead. Their accounts were compared with the accounts of another group of patients that had not experienced an NDE. The researchers were therefore able to analyze the effects and causes of the near-death experience. The results of this investigation dismissed the theory which holds that NDEs are caused by lack of oxygen to the brain. If this were the case, all of those included in the survey should have experienced the NDE phenomenon, when in fact only 18% of those interviewed had done so. The research also dispelled the notion of medication-induced "hallucinations" of the dying brain, for these drugs did not affect the likelihood of experiencing an NDE, nor did they affect the depth of the experience. Of the 344 patients involved in the study, 18% reported a memory stemming from a flatlined state, and 12% recalled a full-blown NDE.

In order to evaluate their experience, individuals scored points based upon Dr. Kenneth Ring's list of NDE criteria, which was published in his 1980 book *Life at Death: A Scientific Investigation of the Near-Death Experience.* In subsequent follow-ups, it was discovered that the NDErs recalled their experience with the same amount of clarity and detail provided in their original accounts.

Additional research has been carried out by Dr. Peter Fenwick, a highly respected British neuropsychiatrist and Fellow of the Royal College of Psychiatrists, who has studied more than three hundred NDEs over the last forty years. He too questions the brain-based NDE theories, because he argues that when the brain is effectively dead, it cannot register conscious experience. The true explanation for NDEs, he believes, could lie in the existence of consciousness beyond the brain. Dr. Fenwick suggests there may well be a spiritual dimension to NDEs, and made the following statement at the 2004 Annual Conference of the International Association for Near-Death Studies (an organization formed in 1981):

A major and relatively rapid shift is underway in the field of medicine. In the past 10 years, medical professionals have gone from looking upon spirituality with a skeptical eye, to embracing it enthusiastically. *Journal of Near-Death Studies,* Spring 2005.

The International Association of Near-Death Studies (known as IANDS) has grown into a large organization with local chapters in the United States and throughout the rest of the world. It was founded as a forum for NDE discussion and research, with a membership comprised of both professionals and laypersons. Accounts of NDE's are of great interest to the public at large, for they are inspirational and spiritually uplifting. Survivors of such experiences share their certainty and belief in a continuum of consciousness, as the soul or essence leaves the body at the time of physical death.

When these individuals return to "normal" life, they are permanently changed, and exhibit the deep commitment to which Plato referred — acting with justice and love in their dealings with others. In the opinion of NDE survivors, love is the only worthwhile and enduring quality in the afterlife, and it is the wisdom of recognizing this Truth that enables true love to blossom in all of its beauty and glory on the earthly plane.

The Dutch researchers performed a follow-up, interviewing the same patients several years after the initial study. All of the patients exhibited greater empathy and acceptance of others following their NDE, and each was far more appreciative of life. Those studied had also lost all fear of death and the process of dying.

Dr. Pim van Lommel, who conducted the research, believes that NDEs are challenging the theory that consciousness ceases at the moment of physical death, for although the patients in his study were certified to be clinically dead, they reported memories of consciousness in which they could perceive events that were actually taking place above and outside of their "dead" bodies.

Cardiologist, Dr. Michael Sabom, conducted a detailed investigation into NDEs, and published his findings in a book entitled *Light and Death*. Initially, he didn't accept that "there was such a thing as a near-death experience." Dr. Sabom first encountered stories about people who had died — and supposedly witnessed glimpses of another form of existence — in the accounts collected by Raymond Moody in his book *Life After Life*. After hearing a talk on Moody's findings, Sabom's response was, "I don't believe it." Nevertheless, he was persuaded to prepare a report for interested parties in a Methodist Church, and decided to interview several of his own patients to see if any of them had experienced such a phenomenon. He fully expected a negative response that would endorse his skeptical viewpoint, but was amazed when several of his patients related NDEs. As he listened to one of these accounts, and felt the deep and genuine emotion with which the patient related her story, his doubt became replaced with the idea that there must be more to Moody's stories. Sabom realized that Moody had no scientific evidence to back up his claims, and so decided to carry out his own research to substantiate Moody's findings.

During his investigations, Sabom highlighted a particularly dramatic account of an NDE occurring while the individual was brain-dead. Pam Reynolds clinically died in a procedure known as a "standstill." Her temperature was lowered and blood was removed from her brain, effectively rendering her brain-dead. During the ensuing operation, she had an out-of-body experience. After the operation, she was able to describe events (later confirmed by others) about which she could have had no previous knowledge. She also experienced a full-blown NDE, which completely transformed her life. Dr Sabom considers this case to be the most influential in his extensive NDE "Atlanta Studies" and, over the years, he has come to the conclusion that the near-death experience could take place while the soul is detaching from the physical body during the dying process.

Dr. Elisabeth Kubler-Ross, one of the great pioneers in the field of death and dying, carried out her own extensive research into the then little-known NDE phenomenon. In her book *The Wheel of Life: A Memoir of Living and Dying*, she relates how one of her patients, a Mrs. Schwartz, recounted such an experience shortly before making her final transition. This was the first time Kubler-Ross had encountered such an occurrence. After hearing Mrs. Schwartz's story, Kubler-Ross became convinced that many other people must have experienced the same phenomenon. She then decided to interview her other patients, with the idea that investigating NDEs could help shed light upon and expand our limited understanding of what happens to consciousness at the moment of death.

Kubler-Ross was astounded at the results of her findings: many of her patients related personal accounts of NDEs. One woman, who had lost her sight in an accident, described how she had regained her vision during her near-death experience, and was able to describe everything that had taken place in great detail.

During an NDE, the being of Light who often meets and guides visitors to the after-death realm is viewed in the personal or cultural religious/mythic background of the individual undergoing the experience. This is also the case with death-bed visions — sometimes referred to as awareness-of-death experiences or threshold-of-death experiences — which can occur when a person is approaching death, or is just about to die. Worldly concerns slip away and a psychic sensitivity is activated, so that visions of an apparent afterlife are clearly seen.

A near-death experience may include some or all of the following:

- looking down on one's inert body
- cessation of pain
- a feeling of peace
- seeing a tunnel and being drawn into it
- the sound of beautiful music
- glimpsing a bright light in the distance
- arriving at a heavenly place suffused in light and feeling unconditional love and acceptance

- meeting departed relatives and/or a divine/mystical being
- a life review
- wise counseling

Some NDEs are extremely vivid, and contain all the above elements. It is also possible to have a more superficial experience that nonetheless carries a powerful message. It's been documented that a comparatively small number of negative NDEs take place; these have been described as being extremely disturbing and frightening. There are also cases of individuals who have clinically died and been resuscitated, but have no memory of experiencing an NDE. Why the disparity?

Swiss psychiatrist C.G. Jung, the great pioneer of the psychoanalytic movement experienced many dreams about death and dying. In 1944, he had an NDE, during which he experienced a life review and a vision of the entire cosmos, and saw the reality of other realms of consciousness. Jung was told that he must return to earth and, like many NDE survivors, he felt enormous disappointment at having to return to everyday life. Still, he emerged from this life-changing event having undergone what he described as an "inner transcendent experience." From that moment on, his work gained a fresh perspective.

Jung suggested that our inner sense of connectedness and higher purpose — reflected in the perspective of the *imago dei* (image of God), and referred to as the spiritual or wholistic archetype or spiritual instinct — often remains unconscious. But it is always there, urging us to discover our true reality. A negative NDE may act as a shocking wake-up call, modifying a way of thinking and behavior that has caused the individual to live an "unlived life" devoid of meaning and lacking any form of authenticity. In some instances, the fearful experience has become a benign one, as the person calls out to a higher source for help and guidance. A positive experience may be seen as an affirmatory thinking and behavior-enhancer. Some individuals, experiencing NDEs after suicide attempts, returned with a new sense of direction and appreciation for life, abandoning further thoughts of suicide.

Those who have died and come back to life with no memory of an NDE may not have progressed far enough into the altered, NDE state of consciousness to imprint a lasting recall. For some people, perhaps, an occurrence of such archetypal proportions cannot be integrated into conscious awareness.

In death we must let go of the restrictive concepts of "me and mine" with which most people identify. This includes our physical bodies. Other worldly identities must also be abandoned when dying. But how much better it would be to voluntarily relinquish these ego-based attachments while still alive, so that we can relate more lovingly to those around us, rather than constantly dwelling between joy and misery.

Will greater public awareness of NDE and its implications serve to positively affect behavior? Plato, in his time, believed that it could. Today, veteran researchers like Dr. Kenneth Ring still hold this to be true. In his book *Lessons from the Light*, he cites his study of a number of NDErs, and a control group of non-NDErs known to be interested in the subject. He discovered that the control group, "reflected the same kind of values profile" as the NDEr group, though usually less intensely.

The control group's belief and value changes developed after their interest in the NDE phenomenon began. One individual who had a near-death experience featured in the book explained that, "You don't have to die to get there." But, as Plato commented, you do have to practice!

The implications of NDE are of profound significance, for they foster an unshakable conviction in the connectedness of all beings, and the reality of life after death. The survivors of such an event often find it painful to return to their body and leave the bliss they experienced during their temporary sojourn in the afterlife. Many find it difficult to integrate their NDE, and cannot speak about it openly, as friends and family can be unsympathetic and refuse to discuss what has taken place. On occasion, the individual is left to cope alone with the magnitude of what they have witnessed. Some are afraid of being shunned or ridiculed, as relatives start to become fearful and believe them to be suffering from some form of mental breakdown. Organizations such as IANDS, however, offer such people a safe environment in which to discuss and share their profound revelations with fellow NDErs, who can help them come to terms and validate their experience.

These people return to everyday reality totally transformed, with a new awareness of their unique destiny and purpose, and often with a mission to fulfill in this lifetime. They are inspired to make great changes in their lives, and these changes prove to be permanent. They are all convinced that "Love" abounds, with its feelings of ecstasy and deep bliss, and that this is the most important message to share with their fellow beings. This resonates with the concepts of *Prema* (unconditional divine love), *Leela* (the divine play of consciousness), and *Ananda* (divine bliss) from the spiritual traditions of India in particular, but with other mystical traditions of the world as well. When a life-embracing love becomes the essence of our living, the truly miraculous core of existence may be continually experienced.

Like the shaman or medicine man of ancient indigenous cultures, who possessed the ability to enter a trance and cross the threshold between life and death, NDE survivors also return from a euphoric journey, often endowed with enhanced psychic, intuitive and healing abilities.

The new life values exhibited by NDErs are not always easy to practice in our materially-driven world, but the stories of their experiences serve as an example to others. While it is true that many have become inspired to practice similar principles through religious traditions, the sense of spiritual universality and compassion for all — including those outside of a particular religious belief system — is often absent.

In a world where the concept of the connectedness of all beings, respect for nature, compassion toward all life forms and a belief in a higher sense of purpose have become replaced by doubt, fear, ecological disasters, war and violence, the near-death experience serves as a modern day myth. It provides a foundation for remythologizing our beliefs about the meaning of existence, and for expanding our consciousness until we remember or rediscover long-forgotten truths. Such truths have been handed down from the oral traditions and sacred texts to shed light on the mystery of birth, death and rebirth into a continuum of consciousness. By studying examples of temporary visits to the afterlife, it becomes possible to remember that exile and homecoming are part of our current mythology, because NDE provides a means to encounter the archetype of wholeness, and to access the meaning of existential consciousness. For as Plato states at the end of the *Republic:*

> Given what Er has reported about the next world, it looks as though not only will he be happy here, but his journey from here to there and back again won't be along the rough underground path, but along the smooth heavenly one.

The near-death experience also provides depth psychologists with a model to work from in helping the many alienated individuals who face crisis and fragmentation of the personality. As Helen M. Luke points out in *Dark Wood to White Rose:*

> Our sickness is fundamentally due to the breakdown of the symbolic life which all the great religions have existed to maintain, so that we are left with eyes that see not and ears that hear not beyond the literal facts and voices of our environment…and our inner ear is deaf to the song of angels.

The profound insights gained through the NDE can be psychologically adapted to illustrate the concept of letting go of a limited identification with the outer façade and maladaptive patterning, resulting in deep healing and the reemergence of the "true" self. Jung described this path to wholeness as being the individuation process, a state in which the individual reconnected with nature and a supreme consciousness. The mythic journey of initiation, symbolic death, and rebirth is extensively detailed in Joseph Campbell's book, *The Hero with a Thousand Faces*. As Campbell states:

> Only birth can conquer death – the birth, not of the old thing again, but of something new. Within the soul, within the body social, there must be – if we are to experience long survival – a continuous "recurrence of birth"…to nullify the unremitting recurrences of death.

The personal accounts of NDEs presented in the following stories demonstrate how each of the individuals featured was empowered and gained wisdom from the experience. The lives of all have been transformed, and the group is part of a growing number of people moving through the world in a state of higher consciousness. These narratives illustrate that it is possible to lead a more authentic life, in which we remember how to live in sacred communion with the natural world.

The following survivors of NDE have lost all fear of the dying process, and are spiritually prepared to accept death and even welcome it. Their apprehension of journeying into unknown territory has diminished, through understanding that our essential nature can never die, and that the impermanent part of us — our physicality — is a temporary manifestation of being that ebbs and flows like a tide. Embracing these truths results in a renewed zest for living, and heralds a return to a state of unbounded awareness – which is eternal.

These individuals have returned from this threshold with increased intuitive, psychic and healing abilities, and live their lives in service to others. They have all experienced what Jung refers to as moments of "absolute knowledge" about the true meaning of life, and are actively engaged in the practice of conscious living and dying. As Socrates states in Plato's *Phaedo*, "all the true philosophers…are always occupied in the practice of dying, wherefore also to them least of all men is death terrible."

In Larry's story, his NDE-like experience was the result of raising consciousness through the use of LSD, in the days when it was legal to use and various clinical tests in Europe and America had proved the drug to be of therapeutic value. The powerful effects of LSD resulted in an altered state of awareness that could be illuminating, and give rise to spiritual and religious symbolism which provided profound insights and answers to existential questions. Although problems would develop in some "casual" cases of LSD use, Larry's experiment was carefully conducted under the guidance of those who knew how to implement the proper safeguards. Larry's experience shares a number of similarities with near-death, out-of-body, and certain shamanic otherworldly journeys. He transcended the familiar but too often limited confines of the body and body-orientated consciousness, and came to understand that death was just another stage of our development and we go on to different levels of existence.

All of the people featured in the following pages are certain that a higher power resonates in our lives, giving rise to meaningful coincidences or "synchronicities." They are assured that life has a purpose, and they have gained an utter belief that beyond physical death, life continues in another form of consciousness. They have "practiced dying," and unraveled the mystery of Plato's dying words, providing an example for others to follow.

REUBEN'S STORY

Death may be the greatest of all human blessings
Socrates

Reuben's calm assurance that death is merely a transition to be embraced, and not feared, gives people in the dying process hope and strength. There is a quality of being that makes you feel alive when you're around him. Doubts slip away, and the eternal presence from which all things arise becomes a living reality that echoes in the pulse of your own heartbeat.

It's a beautiful late spring day in the Ojai Valley. The vibrancy of nature can be felt all around Meditation Mount, a beautiful property in the east end of the valley, from which the teachings of Alice Bailey are disseminated. Reuben seems remarkably attuned to the environment, and very appreciative of it. He points out birds and flowers, and knows each of their names. He has a love for what he sees that is palpable, and his sensitivity is contagious. Looking far ahead, to a wooded area across the valley, he says that he can sense people walking there. It's impossible to see anyone in the trees at that distance, but he is soon proven right: a few minutes later, the hikers enter a clearing.

* * * * *

Reuben

When I was thirteen years old, I decided there was no purpose to my life, much less power of purpose. But I did have a firm resolve — to commit suicide. I was unconcerned about any idea of an afterlife, and didn't believe there was one. Ending my life was something I had thought about, and it seemed an obvious decision. I was physically and emotionally abused, and sensed my mother didn't want me. We were also struggling financially as a family, and I believed myself to be a burden. My grand-mother was raising me, and she was already ninety-seven. There was nothing to look forward to and nobody to connect with; there seemed no reason to carry on living. It was an easy decision to make. I locked myself in the bathroom, disconnected the hose from the old gas heater, put a towel over my head, lay down and waited to die.

I felt myself floating away and entering a very dark tunnel, and I could see lights flashing by me, but I could only concentrate on this tiny light on the horizon. I was flying incredibly fast, and then popped out of the tunnel into…light! In the distance, there was a fence with a gate. An old man was opening the gate. He was communicating with me, but no words were spoken. "You can come and look," was the message he conveyed. There was a lake of water between us, which seemed to be blocking my way, but then I immediately found myself standing next to him. He floated off to the left, as I started to hear the most beautiful music playing, and then suddenly the old man had vanished. There was only a field of flowers stretching as far as the eye could see. The colors were so majestic, and as I gazed at one of the flowers, I realized it was their color that was singing and making the music.

It was all so beautiful. For the first time I was totally loved and a part of everything; this was my home. I didn't want to be anywhere else. This love was unconditional, something that I had never experienced before. I was loved just as I was.

Then I felt myself floating up again and as the field of flowers disap-peared, I heard the sound of flowing water. People were coming towards me and communicating how glad they were to see me. My heart was full of happiness, and I wanted to race over in their direction, but found that I couldn't move. Most of them looked at me lovingly, and then carried on with their activities, except for one woman. She was slim and beautiful, and wore a distinctive old-fashioned dress. I felt strongly drawn to run towards her. But an immensely powerful light came between us, and I "heard" the words, "You cannot touch her - you must not reach out to her," and she faded away.

Then another entity approached and advised me: "This is not the right way to come here."

"No," I replied, "I know this isn't the way."

The "voice" continued, saying, "It's not time for you yet; you have to go back."

Immediately, I was back in my body, and I could hear my grandmother banging on the bathroom door. Somebody else was trying to break in through the window. I was taken to the doctor, but have no conscious memory of what happened there.

I tried to talk to my grandmother about my experience, only to be told, "You must never mention this to anyone — just put it out of your mind." She was, however, intrigued by the woman I described, and would keep asking me questions about her. I refused to answer, but years later learned that she had been my aunt, the daughter of my grandmother, who had died prior to my birth.

I was convinced that my experience was real, in spite of what others thought, and now knew for certain that unconditional love existed, and that I had been sent back for a purpose and had something important to accomplish.

Forty years passed. I established a financially rewarding career in real estate and banking. Although conscientious in my working life towards my clients, my first priority was to myself and the company I worked for. I wasn't a very fulfilled person. Somehow, the unconditional love experienced in my NDE seemed to be in short supply. My energy was channeled into leading the life of a workaholic, and along the way I had managed to survive two failed marriages. My lifestyle made me a prime candidate for a heart attack, but I took no notice of the signals my body was giving me. One Saturday morning, I felt an immense pain around my chest, and was forced to go to the doctor for a check-up. He informed me that I was experiencing minor heart attacks.

"We need to get you to a hospital immediately for more tests," he said.

"I'll drive you over there."

"No," I replied. "I have an important meeting to attend. This will have to wait until later."

Very reluctantly, he administered some nitroglycerine and wrote out a prescription for me to get filled. "You must take this immediately," he said, "before you do anything else, and you must go to hospital as soon as you have finished your meeting."

I agreed in order to pacify him, but then just jumped straight into my car and got back to work; the hospital check-in could wait. Arriving home that evening, my heart couldn't wait, as I was once more struck by an explosive, paralyzing pain. I was in bad trouble, and was alone. The nearest phone was in the living room, which now seemed a hundred miles away. With great difficulty, I started the long journey down the hallway from the bedroom. After a few faltering steps, I doubled over and bumped against the wall and watched the floor come up to hit my face. I must have blacked out in mid-air, and never felt the impact.

I came round in total darkness, straining to see and wondered, "What's happening here? There must be some light from the street or the living room." But there was nothing other than an eerie silence. Stranger still, I had lost all sense of feeling and upon trying to call out, discovered that I couldn't make a sound. I began to feel terrified and thought, "Oh God, I don't belong in this place," and started to pray for help.

Then I saw a flash of light, like a spark coming off a flint, and off in the distance, I detected a tiny flicker like a candle flame. The thought I repeated to myself was, "Don't blow out — don't blow out." Instantly, two more lights appeared and as they moved closer, I saw they had human forms.

One of the beings said, "We've come a long way for you."

I thought, "Thank goodness help has finally arrived."

I was escorted upwards by the beings and out of the dark abyss. We were moving very fast, as the three human-shaped lights were communicating with me. Although it was difficult to really understand them, I knew they were imparting important information, as intense waves of love washed over my whole being. Then I became aware of myriads of other lights, just like me.

We were all heading in the same direction and one of the beings told me:

"You're going back home; you're going back to God."

All the lights were merging together, as I began to witness the start of creation and the beginning of life. The darkness began to recede and a brilliant light started to take its place; it appeared as a mountain of numinous light, like a crystal shining across the entire sky. Although brighter than the sun, I could look directly into its radiant depths.

Then a voice said, "Now you know that everything is love," and the voice itself was love, as it whispered, "You're one of mine." The feelings of bliss and ecstasy were overwhelming and as the light penetrated me, I knew there was nothing but light and that the darkness was only an illusion.

Music started to play, the music I had longed to hear again and, in an instant, a life review was laid out before me. My entire past flashed before me — all the people I had touched, and all the things I had changed just by existing on the planet earth. It wasn't so much about anything I had said or done in my life; it was all to do with simply being there, and being a part of everything that had been created. I understood that I was connected to everything that exists in the universe. The colors were pulsating, and the music sounded magnificent. I knew this was my real home.

But the voice interrupted this wonderful euphoria saying, "Your work is not done."

I protested, and replied, "Not done? You mean I have to go back?"

Just as I felt that I couldn't bear such a let-down, I found myself on the floor of my apartment, in terrible pain. My clock read 4:45 a.m. More than five hours had elapsed, and the phone was mysteriously off the hook, as an operator's voice repeated, "Don't hang up; help is on the way."

I heard sirens and a great commotion of clanging and banging, and then I was floating up near the ceiling looking down at seven people working on my body. I tried to shout, "Leave that body alone; don't touch it," but nobody could hear me.

I was aware of what they were saying though, and could see what they were doing. Later I talked to four EMTs about what took place. They were astonished; they told me that I had been totally unconscious and that there was no plausible way for me to have any knowledge of the events I related to them.

As the paramedics continued working on me, I started to drift away and could hear someone outside the building calling my name. The neighbors had gathered out on the street and immediately I was right in the middle of them, listening to their conversation, and was aware of their innermost feelings.

Then my thoughts turned towards my brother, who was up in Oregon. All at once, I was in his house, listening, watching and feeling, while he and his wife were in the kitchen. It was an awkward situation. He was going on a fishing trip, and she was unhappy about it. She wasn't talking to my brother; she was having this dialogue with herself about what she would do when he was gone. Afterwards, they both confirmed that the scene had taken place exactly as I had described it.

Next, I found myself back in California and inside an ambulance, which was speeding along with the siren blaring. I was still not in my body, but was in the instrument panel looking at all the little colored wires, and also trying to tell the driver the best route to the hospital. There was a fork in the road, and I knew instinctively that we should turn left, even though I had never been to the hospital before. While I was still in the ambulance, I could see what was going on in the emergency room, and watched the medical team prepare to work on me.

Once my body had arrived at the hospital, a nurse started to thump my chest, as another inserted an IV. I tried to insist that they left me alone, but they lifted me onto the operating table and hooked me up to all sorts of equipment. This was the moment when I reentered my body.

Upon regaining physical consciousness, medical personnel urged me to sign a consent form agreeing to immediate surgery to unblock my arteries. Knowing intuitively what I had to do, I said, "I can't. I can't destroy my body; I have to finish my work." I couldn't explain to them all I had gone through in my near-death experience. Eventually, they gave up trying to convince me to have the surgery, and I was sent home with a shopping bag full of drugs. Before leaving, however, the surgeon admonished me saying, "You'll be back within three months, and you won't have a choice about the operation." But somehow, I wasn't worried.

I returned home and started to recuperate. After a few weeks, I remembered that I'd been sent back to accomplish something, and knew there was work left to do, but had no clue as to what it was supposed to be. I was staring into the bathroom mirror and said, "God I can't do the job. I don't know what to do." A response came immediately, "It's the drugs; get rid of them. The medication is blurring your mind." I followed the instructions, and just threw them all away.

At a check-up the doctor was shocked by my action. He said, "You can't stop those drugs cold turkey. They're potent and you need to wean yourself off them." However, he couldn't deny that things seemed absolutely fine. He carried out some tests, and much to his amazement, everything was back to normal, although he stated his categorical belief that I would never work again with my preexisting condition. But I knew otherwise, for I had discovered a new profound sense of purpose to carry out my still unknown mission.

There was nothing much to do while recuperating except to read the newspapers and watch T.V. I was aware from the news that several prominent people had died of heart attacks, which led me to wonder, "Why them and not me?" I remembered the awful feeling of being alone in my apartment, when I was dying, and thought, "There must be a lot of people who don't have anyone with them when they die." In a flash I understood. This was the work the omniscient Voice had sent me back to do. I was immediately sure of it, and instantly knew that this work and service would provide me with the means to manifest the love experienced in my NDE, which I now understood was at the heart of everything.

I had some savings to live on and moved into a new apartment. Then, shortly after, a neighbor invited me to attend a lecture on practical spirituality. While attending the meeting, I noticed a brochure describing the Nightingale Project that provided services to the dying. I was interested in contacting them, but didn't follow up. Some time later, I went to an unrelated event and, to my considerable surprise, discovered that Project Nightlight had its office in the same building. After meeting with the Director, I began volunteer work with the dying.

In the course of this work, I met a lady called Susan Storch, an R.N. she had studied all aspects of conscious living and dying and care for the dying, at a private university near Los Angeles. The school, founded by Dr. Benito Reyes, was spreading the word about NDEs and the existence of the afterlife. They had been bridging the gap between science and spirituality through conferences featuring renowned workers and researchers in the field, such as Drs. Kubler-Ross, Moody, and Ring. I now felt certain that I needed to include this same indispensable dimension in my own work, and so completed their thanatology program.

A few years later, I was the volunteer coordinator at the Encino Hospice. There was a young man whom I had been visiting for about three months, and he had taken a turn for the worse. My office was only ten minutes from the hospice, so I visited him after work. We talked for about an hour, but then he grew tired and needed to sleep. The nurse who was on duty agreed to call me before her shift ended, in order to let me know how Johnny was doing.

The following morning, I woke up with an urgent feeling to return to the hospice, even though I had not been called. When I arrived, Nurse Mary advised me that Johnny was not waking up. I called out his name to let him know that I was at his side. He tried to open his eyes, but was too weak. His breathing was very shallow and his hand was cool when I took it in my hand. I told him not to be afraid, to relax and feel all the love waiting for him. I felt Mary come into the room and stand behind me.

I motioned to Mary not to speak, as I continued to tell Johnny that he would not be alone at any time and would find love and peace. There was a tear slowly rolling down his cheek, as he took a deep breath. Then his face turned light and there was a palpable surge of energy and an essence of many colors that lifted and faded away. Johnny never exhaled, and I thanked him for letting me come to say farewell. Both Mary and I felt and saw the kaleidoscope of colors that formed Johnny's aura. This was not an isolated experience, but was one of the more memorable, which confirmed that there is so much more for us to learn.

Today, I work full time as a spiritual counselor and thanatologist at the Roze Room hospice in Los Angeles. I am also the facilitator for the Los Angeles Chapter of the International Association for Near-Death Studies — an organization devoted to research and education pertaining to all aspects of NDE, which also offers support to those who may have a difficult time integrating their experience, and to individuals who may want to know more about the subject.

When people ask me to share my beliefs following my illuminating NDE, I describe them in the following way: We all get attached to our physical bodies, but it isn't the deepest truth of who we are. People don't enjoy life, because they worry all the time — about material possessions, about the future, about something they want or don't want. It's a funny thing: we strive for perfection in our lives, but we don't realize that perfection already exists, and that we don't have to go searching for it. The secret lies in reversing our usual order of business that is always striving to become something more; instead, we can try to experiment with becoming less and less, until we are nothing at all. Then we will discover an amazing truth: in reality, we are everything.

My job as a spiritual counselor is to help dying people and their families understand that the body is merely clothing for the soul. When it is discarded, we move on to a wonderful place that is awaiting our arrival.

As death approaches, many people are asking for a miracle, and I tell them, "Death is the miracle you're looking for."

* * * * *

Reuben has an extraordinary presence and in some mysterious way, he has glimpsed the soul's final destination into a continuum of consciousness. As he finishes narrating his story, dusk is beginning to fall over the valley. The sun becomes a huge orange globe, setting in a clear blue sky. High above, fingers of pink light begin to softly caress the surrounding mountaintops. It is easy in this moment to imagine the miracle of creation, and begin to view death of the physical body in a different way: not as a heart-wrenching struggle to fight our way through, but as part of a journey through eternity.

TIFFANY'S STORY

...from the door in the heavens souls came down pure
Plato

Tiffany Snow had an NDE after being struck by a lightning bolt. During her experience, she was "welcomed to the world of healers." At the time, she had no idea of what this meant. Following her recovery, she went to attend to her horse, Stars, who was suffering from a chronic skin ailment. Having run out of the prescribed medication, she just rubbed his belly around the outside of the infection, and noticed that her hands had become very hot. After repeating a similar treatment, Stars completely recovered. This was the first sign that God had blessed her with the gift of healing.

Every day, about 2,000 thunderstorms create lightning somewhere over the earth. The chance of being struck by a lightning bolt is roughly 1 in 700,000. The electrical discharge strikes with a powerful force, which can cause death or serious injury. In Greek mythology, thunder and lightning were bestowed upon the sky-god Zeus, and were used by him to rule over the mortal and immortal realms. Thunder was also deemed to symbolize the absolute ruling power that ascended from deep within the rumblings of the earth to heaven, and was often referred to symbolically as the "voice of God." Lightning reflected the message of the Gods that was written in the sky, and was recognized as a symbol of spiritual enlightenment. Survivors of a lightning strike may not necessarily recall an NDE, but it is interesting to note that most of them return to everyday consciousness with enhanced psychic and telepathic abilities.

* * * * *

Tiffany

It was a stormy, rainy day in Tennessee. I stood at the corral, worried about my horses — especially Stars, who was out in the pasture. Out of the dark-laden sky came a flash and immediately before losing consciousness, I realized that I had been struck by lightning. Fortunately, I had been holding on to a barbed-wire fence with one hand and a wet wooden pole with the other, so the charge passed on through my body. Still, it was enough to kill me.

I just remember doing an uncontrollable electrical "dance," as my muscles contorted. I felt no pain and in a split second, I turned around and tried to push my chest against the corner of the parked truck, knowing that electrical shocks often stop at the heart. Then my eyesight narrowed and I felt my body slowly slide down the bumper onto the wet earth and everything turned black...

I found myself standing way up in the universe, surrounded by distant colorful planets. I could see misty pinpoints of stars through my right arm and when I moved it back and forth, the stars rippled like a reflection on water. I felt dizzy and had a sense of being able to see not only in front of me, but all around me, at the same time. Floating just a few feet away, I saw a man with a spirit body just like mine, although he was short and had slanted eyes. He spoke to me in a "voice" that I could hear inside my head, saying: "Don't be afraid."

On the other side of me, another spirit person, who was much taller and had chiseled facial features, nodded approvingly. All the while, we were moving very fast towards a ball of spinning light; it was brilliant white in the middle and yellowish around the outside edges. The closer we got to it, the more I felt an overwhelming Love that seemed so warm and comforting, as it encompassed my total being.

We stopped. The bright light was still some distance away. I wanted to move on and felt like a magnet irresistibly drawn to this source. The desire to merge with the light became stronger as we got closer, and I knew this place was the heavenly throne of God himself.

I couldn't understand why we had come to a standstill. I became confused, yearning to reach the Great Almighty, who was beyond my reach. Then a glowing luminousness appeared in front of me. Gold and white sparkles merged in a glowing spiritual body to form a giant image in the shape of a man, with broad shoulders. A Divine Presence stood before me.

A gentle voice called out from this realm of golden sparkles saying, "What have you learned?" The voice was so soft and tender, and yet the presence of Divine Authority was there; I knew it was the voice of the son of God, the empowered Jesus Christ.

Instantly, a life review unfolded before my very eyes. Key moments when I had shown anger or love towards people appeared like scenes out of a movie. I could feel the hurt of those I had been mean to and saw how these negative feelings had a domino effect, as they spread on through others. I also experienced the love I had shared with people, and how much further that rippled out and connected me to all things that were wonderful and blessed. I had never before experienced such joy.

Then the presence of Christ said: "The Flesh is the Test of the Spirit...Love Each Other." As I heard these words, I felt overwhelmed with love, and so privileged.

I wanted to stay! I wanted to join God's swirling life force. I wanted to feel more Love, but was not allowed to go any further. I listened expectantly, just waiting for him to speak again and I faintly heard voices singing the most beautiful melody. I knew it was the sound of angels and those joined with God, and that this heavenly choir came from the Swirling Brilliant Presence.

I couldn't make out the meaning of the words and felt very sad, because I knew that I had to return to earth and make a "better movie." At that moment, I vowed to carry out the will of this Divine Presence, and surrendered all my earthly desires. Instantly, I felt a child-like sense of wonderment, as a feeling of bliss and peace filled my entire being. A warm tingling sensation washed over me like warm liquid honey flowing from the top of my head down to my toes. I wondered what was happening. Later, I discovered that this kind of experience is referred to as the baptism of the Holy Spirit, an anointing more commonly experienced on earth. At that moment everything became crystal clear: I would spend the rest of my earthly life in service and carry out the will of this Powerful Loving God. Now, I had a mission.

The spirit on my right then telepathically communicated again and answered many of my questions. He also shared details of many wonderful and sacred things. While I was floating before the Christ Consciousness, the spirit then told me something that I didn't understand; he said, "Welcome to the world of healers." This was a shock, for although I had been ordained in 1979, I belonged to a church that believed healing had died out in the first century, and that NDE's were caused by chemical reactions in the brain. I tried to figure out what all this meant.

At this point, the Christ presence faded away into formless sparkles, and the stars behind his glowing features were visible once more. I was in the midst of such effervescent beauty, and surrounded by many shapes of heavenly bodies transfixed in the cosmos; each one unique and necessary, all of them untold distances away. But at the same time, they seemed close enough to reach out and pluck from the sky.

The slant-eyed spirit continued to teach me even more. He pointed out different stars, planets, distant swirling lights of all kinds, and gave names to all of them. I was given the answers to thousands of questions, and reams of information seemed to be exploding in my head. I wondered whether these things were newly learned, or just remembered. Everything felt so familiar.

Then I felt myself sinking, as if falling through a bed. I woke up to find my husband shaking me by the shoulders. Somehow, my physical body was now lying on the front seat of the truck, although I had left it outside slumped in the mud. Since leaving the house to go to the tractor shed, three hours had elapsed. The storm had passed, but left evidence to show that at least three other strikes had occurred on the pasture, besides the one that had struck me.

In the emergency room, I was hooked up with wires and given tests to monitor my heart, which proved to be undamaged. But my eyes and ears were affected very badly, as was my sense of balance. Although I felt dizzy, I was keenly aware of my experience. I was wearing a single diamond earring, and a brown burn mark encircled the gold part of the stud, where it went through my ear. My skin tingled all over and was extremely sensitive, especially in the areas around my arms and hands.

The doctors told me, "You've been very lucky — often an arm or leg gets blown off during a strike. People frequently die as a result of such an incident." I didn't know if they were joking or not. They reasoned that my survival was due to my holding the chain-link with one hand and the wet wooden pole with the other, enabling the current to pass through me, instead of grounding in my body. I knew they wouldn't believe that this had been a Divine Strike and a wake-up call, which led me into the presence of God. In fact, I'm sure they would have kept me in the hospital a lot longer, probably strapped into a white jacket and placed me in a locked and padded cell!

I spent a few days in bed, oscillating between wild feelings of extreme happiness and unbelievable sadness. I had never felt such a tide of overwhelming emotions. I was glad to have had the experience, but had not wanted to return. I kept re-living the event over and over, for every detail was emblazoned on my mind. I tried to paint what I had seen, but no matter how the colors were mixed, they were not brilliant enough to recapture the profound enormity of my experience. I felt confused and asked myself, "What does this all mean?"

Soon, I was back to my chores, which included putting salve on Stars skin infection. For six weeks, I had smoothed on the medication that the vet had prescribed, but still the red blisters kept spreading until they had created a bald patch around his girth. The ointment had run out, so I just rubbed Stars' belly lightly around the outside of the sore spot. My hands were getting very hot; I thought it must be bacteria from the infection.

After washing my hands, the feeling of heat disappeared, and I thought no more about it.

The next day, I discovered that the blisters on Stars' belly had turned white, and that some had just fallen off. I stayed with him and gently massaged the same area, and once more experienced a similar sensation of heat spreading through my fingers. The following morning when I visited Stars, I saw that all the blisters had disappeared, and that new hair was beginning to grow around his bald patch. I put this down to be mere coincidence.

Shortly afterwards, I took my cat to be spayed. The vet said it would take ten days for the stitches to completely heal. The day following surgery, my cat didn't want anything to do with me. But by the second day, she was on my lap as much as possible, and would not leave me alone. Every time I picked her up, I would massage and pet her, and I noticed that my hands kept heating up again. On the third day, she tried pulling out the stitches with her teeth. On the morning of the fourth day, I decided to take a look and see what was happening, and discovered that the skin had healed so well that the stitches were puckering her skin too tightly. I was embarrassed to take her back to the vet, so I carefully cut the threads and pulled them out myself, through skin that bore no sign of a surgical scar! Now, I began to understand what was happening.

I wondered if this newly discovered gift of healing would work on human beings, so I said a prayer and laid my hot hands on various parts of my body. Then I made an appointment with my doctor. A recent mammogram had shown lumps in my breast, and I had also been informed that I had fibroid cysts in my uterus, which needed to be removed through surgery.

I anxiously waited for the test results, which gave me the all clear. The breast lumps and fibroid cysts had completely disappeared! Hesitantly, I started sharing this new gift with my friends — and that's when I started running into trouble, because I was absorbing the pain from their various complaints, and that scared me. I soon became wary of using this healing ability, and thought, "I won't last long doing this work. I must be doing something wrong."

I prayed for understanding and looked to the Bible for guidance; the pages simply fell open to relevant scriptures relating to healing, which seemed to confirm that the gift was genuine, and to be used to help ease suffering. I realized that the NDE had occurred because I had resisted finding my true purpose, and had needed an empirical, first-hand experience to open me up to my true creative nature.

One day, a friend invited me to a Reiki demonstration, which was being held near my home in Nashville. She told me that other people with the ability to heal would be there. I cautiously accompanied her, and met a group of people who were praying and laughing, and ministering the laying-on of hands. I realized that their hands became hot like mine, and was interested to know more. When thumbing through the available literature, I saw a picture of a man, a Christian minister, named Dr. Usui, who had named this ancient healing technique "Reiki," and had practiced it in Japan during the 1800's.

I looked at the likeness and gasped, thinking, "I know this man." This was the spirit with the slanted eyes, who appeared beside me in my NDE! This was the very same man! I was stunned, for God works in very mysterious ways. Armed with this information, I knew what my next step should be, and as soon as I decided to go through the training, the pain I was experiencing was gone. I soon received the Reiki Master degree. Now, I felt energized and euphoric after the healings. Reiki is recognized by the American Medical Association as a complementary alternative therapy. Research has proven that it has consistent and measurable results. Not all Reiki practitioners combine the use of prayer with their healings, so the kind of work I began facilitating could be more accurately described as "Divine Healing."

My NDE enabled me to become an open channel to transmit God's healing energy, and my life has become an adventure and a spirit journey! I get to see cancer disappear, brain tumors shrink, blind eyes see, and deaf ears hear. I can also help bring peace and a calm assurance to those transitioning in death. Along the way, this expansive connection with God has led to other manifestations of spirit, such as miraculous long-distance healings, intuitiveness and psychic visions.

Sometimes during healing sessions, the visions in my mind are so clear that I can readily see through the skin, down past the muscle tendons and right through to the inside of the bones. Through my connection to the source, I know that anything is possible, and I tell people, "expect miracles." However, there are occasions when I intuit that a person is about to make their transition and will not receive a physical healing, because my hands will not get hot. I realize that the individual has made a core decision to go home, and remember the joy and Love from my NDE, and know this isn't a bad thing to have happen. I share my experience with them and with their loved ones, because although we cannot escape physical death, we can be assured that life continues in another form, and this reassurance brings enormous comfort and hope to those in the dying process.

Life is to be lived and I enjoy every day, every moment, and every experience. It totally humbles me to be involved in this kind of work. I'm doing exactly what I should be doing, and am blessed to be working at my clinic, The Divine Wellness Institute, in Escondido, California, as a full-time healer.

Truly, the best thing that happened in my life was almost losing it. Being dead healed my life and bestowed upon me the ability to heal others. Up until that point, I had strong religious convictions, but no spiritual concept of God. I saw him through certain limitations and parameters, which were blown away after my incredible experience of coming into his presence. Everything changed from that moment, and I became aligned with my true sense of purpose.

Through the intervention of spirit, we humans can change the world with a message that never changes — the awareness that there is definitely something greater than ourselves; a presence known by many different names, which has the ability and desire to make a powerful difference in our individual lives

The point I want you to remember from my story is this: you don't have to be struck by lightning, or have a near-death experience to open up, change your life, appreciate each other, or to have a special connection with God. Love is the key that opens the door to everything. Remember, your life-review will be about the love you shared, or didn't share!

* * * * *

During Tiffany's NDE, she was ushered into the presence of a loving Divine presence, and witnessed the reality of the life of the soul after death. In this altered state of awareness, she "died" to her old self and preconceived ideas about life, and was "reborn" with a new understanding of the mystery of creation and the interconnectedness of all beings. Having lost all fear of death, she became free to live life fully, and was endowed with her unique mission as a gifted healer and spiritual teacher. The many testimonies to her subsequent miraculous healing abilities appear to confirm that her supernatural gift emanates from her connection to a higher source that enables such gifts to manifest.

DAVE'S STORY

The soul of man is immortal and imperishable
Plato

Dave Bennett grew up in Arizona. As a child, he listened to the spiritual teachings recounted in stories told by his friend's grandmother. As a result, he thought he had a pretty good idea of how to live his life. But following his near-death experience, he realized that he was walking through life, only dreaming of how it was supposed to be.

The ocean symbolizes the energy of life and primordial creation, from which all things are born and to which they will eventually return. The turning tides represent the transitory phase of earthly existence, and simultaneously present an image of life and death. Venus, the Goddess of Love, emerged from the sea-bed with a string of pearls around her neck, symbolizing the divine feminine energy of life. The sea is also a symbol of the Divine Being and universal life. Master Eckhart, a German mystic, philosopher and theologian who was born in the Middle Ages, referred to the ocean as the "unfathomable sea of the nature of God" that symbolizes birth, transformation, and rebirth. The image of the sea can invite a spiritual exploration of eternity, and dispel the concept of separation between the earthly and heavenly realms of existence. It was the perfect scenario for Dave to witness the ultimate reality of a continuum of consciousness.

* * * * *

Dave

My philosophy as a young adult was simple: it was to enjoy life, learn how to survive, and make your mark to get where you want to be. This set of principles served me well as I became a chief engineer and deep-sea diver on a research vessel. It was the perfect job — I got to see the world, meet new people and experience different cultures. I logged thousands of hours diving underwater, and had my share of close calls. But when my life was threatened, a cool sense of calm would ripple through me. I became addicted to the "adrenaline" rush, and loved the thrill of pushing the limits of my endurance.

On the night of my near-death experience, we had just returned from completing a job on a new submersible, and the representative from this vessel was on board. The sea was so rough that the huge swells made it impossible to enter the small harbor of our home port, because the ship would bottom out at the entrance if a wave broke under her. It was late at night when we dropped anchor a couple of miles offshore, and decided to wait there until the storm broke the next day.

The representative who was on board and a couple of crew members were very anxious to reach the shore to enable them to catch their flights home. They eventually persuaded me and a deck hand to take them back in our inflatable Zodiac.

The Captain recommended that we wear life vests, and we agreed. We were all experienced divers and sub operators and were used to being on the sea and in the water, so we rummaged around in the boatswain locker to find the dusty old vests that had been stowed below.

We checked our position on the radar so that we could plot our course to the harbor, and proceeded to load up everyone's gear. Then we lowered the Zodiac into the ocean; the deck hand went to the stern to pilot the boat, and I took the bow to navigate. The craft had a V-4 engine and could really fly across the water, but it sat very low in the swell and we couldn't see the lights of the distant shore through the troughs of the swirling sea.

It wasn't long before we lost our bearings and tried to adjust our direction. Suddenly, we were falling, as a wave broke beneath us. I shouted to the deckhand, "Turn her around and head back out to sea." The mate had just turned the boat around, when the entire sky grew black, except for a ridge of white foam that was about twenty-five feet above our heads.

We were in a sand bar breaker zone, a mile off shore from the harbor. When I saw the foam, I shouted to everyone, "This is it!" as the wave crashed down on us folding the boat in half from bow to stern. Three of the four inflatable pontoons were ruptured, when the aluminum and fiberglass floor broke apart and the motor snapped off the transom.

I was thrown from the bow into the ocean and the waves spun and tumbled me; it was the most raging violent force that had ever attacked my body. I lost all sense of direction, and the ocean tossed me around like a limp rag doll. When I opened my eyes to blow some bubbles and try to get some idea of which way led up to the surface, the sand and salt burned my eyes so badly that I couldn't even see the bubbles.

I didn't know which way was up, but I felt a pressure in my ears, which meant that I was in very deep water. However, all my years as a diver had taught me not to panic. So, I waited and waited for the old Mae West style life vest to take me to the surface. But the surface never appeared within my reach. As time passed, the burning in my lungs lessened, but I was getting extremely cold.

I could tell my brain was starving for oxygen, as a sort of euphoria came over me. I was aware that I might die, and started to have feelings of regret. I remember thinking, "Well, at least my wife will be taken care of with the insurance check." It seemed like an eternity that I was holding my breath, but finally the euphoria took complete hold of me, as I tried to breathe in the salt water. The last thing I remember was the burning and pain in my lungs that slowly diminished, as I became conscious of the freezing cold and utter darkness.

Slowly, through the darkness, I noticed a light and it began to grow lighter all around me. I couldn't feel my body being tossed and tumbled anymore. I could sense where my body was, but I was not in it. As I started to feel warmer, I felt myself slowly moving to a brighter area within the light. It seemed the natural thing to do, for a feeling of being welcomed home and an incredible sense of love flowed through me. I felt so happy, comfortable and loved.

My physical body was gone. I was becoming light, with no form. I didn't judge these events, but just accepted the change. Then within the light, I could sense three others coming towards me, or I was moving towards them. I wanted to be with them, because they seemed so familiar. They welcomed me; I was overcome with joy and the feeling of finally belonging somewhere, rather than being isolated. More beings appeared, maybe a dozen, and they felt like family.

Before I could communicate with any of them, I started to see flashing images from my life pass before me; they surrounded me like a sphere, and I could see in all directions at once. It's very hard to describe in words the intensity of these images, but I could feel the emotions of others and saw how my actions in this life had affected them. I could sense the joy, happiness, heartaches, disappointments and love that had rippled through to others, as a consequence of my actions. But there were no feelings of judgment from the beings that had gathered around me; they just appeared to be supportive

I felt as though I was reviewing my life, so that I might evolve and grow from this incredible experience. Then the images and feelings changed — they were not from my life, but signified events that would take place in the future. I became disorientated and confused.

These other beings were communicating with me, but not in words, as I felt immersed in immeasurable love and compassion. Then I heard a voice distinctly saying, "This is not your time. You must return." I didn't want to return, and I replied, "Please let me stay." But I was told once again, "This is not your time. You have a purpose."

It's a very humbling experience to be in the presence of the Light and I understood immediately that I must return to my body and continue to live my life. I didn't want to come back; it was far more painful than the act of drowning. The original three of my soul group helped me to reenter my body. It was the hardest thing I have ever had to do. I became aware of my lifeless form suspended in the water, which was still being tumbled and blasted by the force of the sand and waves.

Sailors take the end of a line and weave the ends back into the braids of rope, so that the line will not fray. We call that knotted segment the "bitter" end. And a bitter end of a line had wrapped itself around my arm and was beating my chest. The other end of this rope was attached to the Zodiac. When the next set of waves hit, the rope dislocated my shoulder and thumb and pulled my body to the surface. Three of the air-filled compartments were deflated, but one still had air in it. I followed and watched my body go through this sequence of events. The waves hit so hard that some of the water was discharged from my lungs. My body breathed its first breath, and I was slammed back inside it.

My lungs felt as if they were on fire and my head was throbbing. I would have slipped beneath the surface again, if I had not been tangled up with the boat. I coughed and threw up — then tried to breathe once more. The waves still were pounding me, along with the last air-filled pontoon. In the distance, I could hear voices calling out, "Dave where are you?" My shipmates were looking for me, as they had somehow found a flashlight and gathered around it.

My comrades finally spotted me, and I tried to yell back to them, "Over here!" But the only sound that ventured forth was a feeble squawk. Eventually, they paddled over towards me in what was left of the boat, and dragged me afloat. We were still a mile from the coast. Clinging on to the remains of the Zodiac, we began to kick and swim for the shore.

Once I became untangled from the line, I still had trouble staying above the surface, so I kicked off my boots, but that didn't help much. Next, I struggled out of the life vest and discovered that the lining was shredded and waterlogged. Ironically, it was the life vest that had actually killed me and the "bitter end" that had eventually saved me.

When we landed on the shore, two of my shipmates popped my dislocated arm back into place and I remained in a total state of shock. When I reached home, I was so confused that I started to undress outside the door to our apartment, because I was worried that the sand weighing down my pockets would start to spill out. My wife told me that she had a dream during the night, in which she had a premonition that I was going to die, so when I showed up drenched and a day earlier than expected, she got scared. She repeatedly asked me, "What on earth has happened?" I didn't know how to answer her, and my silence frightened her even more. My body temperature was ice cold, so she started to run a bath to warm me up. Eventually, when I managed to explain what had taken place, she started to get mad and very frustrated. I thought it better not to say anything more about my experience, so I told everyone that Neptune had spit me back, just to make light of the situation.

For the following three days, I stayed connected to the Light and started to feel things differently — I could see the life force in everything: trees, flowers, rocks, animals and people. Part of me was still in shock and experiencing physical pain, as my body started its healing process.

During those three days, I realized that I had been given three incredible gifts during my journey to the other side. The first gift was acceptance. I now had a greater awareness of myself and could accept my strengths and weaknesses; I didn't need to beat myself up over past failures, but instead could learn to become a better human being.

The second gift was tolerance. This was very new to me for, like most people, I thought it was normal to try to change others. But following my NDE, I found myself able to respect other people's beliefs and practices, and I understood that the way I lived my life could affect others, without my having any conscious awareness of this taking place. I now appreciated that each individual was on a unique life path, experiencing the lessons they needed to learn for their growth. Tolerance enabled me to allow them to follow this path, without casting any judgments.

The third gift was an understanding of my personal Truth. I was empowered with an ability to know when I was on track, because my heart would brim over with joy, in a way that echoed the feelings of Love that I experienced in the Light. This was such a powerful sensation and what made it even stronger, was the knowledge that my life had a purpose.

My heart was wide open after experiencing the overwhelming force of this unconditional Love, and I felt the spiritual shock of the profound intensity of the revelations that had been bestowed upon me. I also experienced emotionally painful feelings, because for the first time, I had to face my faults and strengths, with honesty and clarity.

I was afraid of telling anyone what had happened; I knew they would dismiss my story and think that I'd gone crazy. So, I started to process the experience and hid the parts that were too hard for me to integrate into my subconscious mind, where they would not be disturbed for some time

With these three newly acquired gifts, my new life started and I began to change. Having grown up in Arizona, I had gained an understanding of the Native American natural way, and I started once more to commune with nature, in order to gain perspective and understanding. The newly awakened, spiritual voice of my being started to give me information that I had no conscious way of knowing. To begin with, I didn't trust this intuition, so I would continuously argue with the voice but, over a period of time, I grew to trust and depend on it.

I continued to live my life with my newly found Truth for the next ten years. Then I went on a spiritual retreat back in Arizona. My plan was to hike along some of the old trails and enjoy myself.

The first day of the retreat, all the participants were meeting for a morning meditation. I went off alone and walked to a little grotto. My intention was to contemplate and become centered and relaxed. But suddenly, I was back in the Light and began reliving my former experience all over again; this time it was very different, for Spirit was talking directly to me, not just projecting thoughts and information.

When I first experienced my NDE, even though I gained incredible insights, the human questioning part of me found it difficult to accept the connection to a Universal All-Knowing God. I realized that this fact had been repressed within me. As I came out of the meditative state, my heart was once more expanded and fully open. For another three days, I hovered between the Light and my physical existence, as scenes from my NDE flashed before me over and over again.

This was my second transformational experience, and it left me with a certainty that I could reconnect with the Light whenever I chose, and that we can all do this. It's just a question of allowing the mind to become quiet and simply listening, for we are all a part of whatever name we give to God. We are all co-creators in everything that takes place in our lives.

This further understanding caused me to change my own life even more. I realized that I was being called to share my knowledge and experience with others. I started what I now call my Quiet Ministry. People needing help started to seek me out, and answers to their problems were channeled through me from Spirit, often in the form of a spiritual seed of greater awareness and understanding.

I think individuals were drawn to me because they could see the different way that I was now expressing love and compassion, following my connection to the Light. During our human existence, we constantly place conditions around expressing love for our fellow beings; we have expectations, and we expect love in return. But unconditional love doesn't work that way. By living your life with no expectation from others, and unconditionally giving your own love; you can start to experience genuine compassion that people are attracted to.

I had a third transformational experience in November, 2000. During my NDE life review, I was shown parts of my life that I had not yet experienced. Dealing with cancer was one of them. This became a reality, when I was diagnosed with stage 1V lung and bone cancer that was eating away the bones in my spine, and eventually caused my spine to collapse.

The doctors told me, "You have a very poor chance of recovery, and it is probably time to get your affairs in order". This prognosis occurred when I was dealing more with my human side, rather than my spiritual dimension. But because of my experiences in the Light, and through my ministry, acceptance of the illness was immediate.

I found myself returning to my center and becoming balanced. Spirit started to give me information on how to deal with all aspects of a terminal disease, including: the pain, the drug-induced highs and lows, and the mental aspects of healing.

I was shown practices of visualization and meditations that served to relieve the physical pain, and helped to stabilize the emotional anxieties and mood swings. I have been in remission now for five years, and Spirit informed me that my future path was to assist other individuals with terminal illnesses and further the work of my ministry.

Someone asked me recently, "Why do people have to suffer?" This is a very hard question to answer, but if you break it down to the basic level, you see that everyone is interconnected with everyone and everything else. When someone is suffering, their suffering touches and affects all those around them, and we need positive and negative experiences for our spirits to form a balance or equilibrium, so that we can evolve and gain wisdom and compassion.

The lessons I learned from these life-transforming events enabled me to understand that we all choose the path we are on, in order to develop and grow. We all have access to God's Light and Love, and we just have to open up to this understanding to experience it. Everyone is faced with obstacles to overcome, and God hasn't abandoned us when the going gets tough, for each of us is part of his Light and Love.

* * * * *

When we try to understand the mystery of life with our rational minds, we create a veil around it. Dave spends his time sharing what he learned during his life-changing NDE with others, and he encourages people to go with the flow of life with a quality of openness that is receptive, sensitive and loving. He reminds us that contemplating and communing with the natural world is the perfect setting to experience a sense of wonder, awe, and reverence that stimulates the imagination into remembering that connection to the sacred life force can be accessed continuously by everyone, who is open to the possibility. The image of God or a higher power is alive in nature and can be felt all around us: We can hear it in the wind whispering through the trees, and smell it in the intoxicating fragrance of the rose. We can taste it in a mountain waterfall, and feel it swirling in the waves that tumble over the mighty ocean. We can see it in the vine that grows steadily towards the light...

RICHIE'S STORY

The immortality of the soul is demonstrated by many proofs
Plato

As a young man, Richie Arrellano had a promising sports career ahead of him, but his dreams were shattered when he was diagnosed with a serious illness. He became depressed and disillusioned about the true meaning of life, until an out-of-body experience persuaded him there must be more to learn. Subsequently, Richie had a NDE, which expanded his limited knowledge even further. Richie knew that he must return to earthly existence and that he had things to accomplish in this lifetime. Following his illuminating NDE, he developed his unique artistic talent, and through the medium of his art, he was able to help others discover their spirituality.

The town of Santa Paula, California, was established by the Chumash Indians. In earlier days, the area was home to two small villages known as Mapu and Srswa. This sacred land was later given away by the Spanish invaders, and formed Rancho Santa Paula. In the late 1800's, the land was divided up into small farms.

Santa Paula is a beautiful area that is set against a backdrop of gently rolling hills and rugged mountaintops. It is situated in the rich agricultural soil of the Santa Clara River Valley, and became famous for its orange, lemon and avocado groves. It was known as the "Citrus Capital of the World."

* * * * *

Richie

My father was born in Texas, but raised in Mexico, where he became an expert farmer and horse trainer. When I was young, the family moved to

Santa Paula, which was the perfect place for my father to settle and find work; he eventually managed to lease some land and built our own small ranch.

My dad influenced me a great deal when I was young. Some of my best childhood memories are from when we would be out together working on the land. He had a deep affinity with the natural world, which led him to develop a down-to-earth philosophy and spirituality. His example led me to honor God as a visible presence that manifested all around me. Dad would often say: "If you want to talk to God, then just go and connect with a rock or a tree."

As a kid, I felt encouraged to explore the whole idea of spirituality, but this landed me in a lot of trouble at my Catholic school. In the fifth grade, I asked the nun teaching catechism, "Can you tell me who God is?" Her reply was to look at me sternly, smack me, and expel me from the class. I guess this unfortunate episode just led me to try to find my own answers.

My father's advice to succeed in life was: "Work hard, do the best you're capable of, keep an open mind and learn from new experiences." These suggestions made sense to me, so I adopted his philosophy.

I was a very active kid, and loved sports. In the sixth grade at Isbell elementary school, I met John Divine. He taught woodwork and also did some coaching after school. The name Divine was perfect for him, since he had a divine gift for bringing out the best in everyone, and he had an inspired way of doing it. He wasn't my teacher, but he thought of all the kids at school as his students. He developed a great way of discussing values and life choices without boring the kids, through noticing whatever sport they were interested in and taking them to professional games in Los Angeles. How he managed to find the time and money to do this, I don't know, but he did. Since I was particularly interested in football, I was invited to go with him and several other kids to a Ram's NFL game. I still remember the occasion so clearly — it was pure magic because we also got to go to the area where the players boarded the buses, and I couldn't believe these famous athletes were right in front of me.

Then one of them saw our group, and yelled to his teammates, "Hey, here's that Divine man and his kids – time to sign some autographs!" At that moment, my admiration for Mr. Divine went up another notch, as I ended up with a collection of autographs including those of the legendary quarterback, John Unitas, and running back, John Arnett.

On the trip back to Santa Paula, Mr. Divine told me that I had it in me to succeed as an athletic director, and I felt motivated about achieving a good career that would help others as well. Gymnastics came naturally to me, and I went on to win the state championship in high school. This assured that I would have my pick of top college scholarships. It seemed like my easy success was fostering my dreams and making them a reality.

Then, out of the blue, devastating news blew my ideas and plans apart: I was diagnosed with testicular cancer, and had to have a testicle removed when I was seventeen. I had to go to nearby Santa Barbara three days a week for treatment. This signaled the end of my sports activities, and the end of my vision of my future career. The illness also led to a period of depression, because it also meant that I would never be able to have children of my own. I felt as though I was a boy on the brink of manhood that seemed to have been cruelly snatched away.

I started to channel some of the energy that I had used on the sports field into art, and gradually began to develop some skills. I started to paint a portrait of John Divine, because even though I wasn't able to realize the career he saw for me, I never forgot his kindness and interest. But my new awareness of the fact that serious illness and death could occur at any time, no matter how healthy you believed yourself to be, led me to adopt the, "eat, drink and be merry, for tomorrow you may die" philosophy. I started to become a major partier, and even organized large-scale events with bands, food, alcohol and the works. It took years for me to realize that this behavior was slowly killing me, even though I didn't seem to be suffering from any particular disease. Then, I discovered that my two sisters had much worse problems.

When I was about twenty-seven, I found out that one of my sisters had become a heroin addict. The whole family was stunned at the news, but my mother was totally devastated and guilt-ridden, even though it was not her fault. My father managed to deal with this situation, in keeping with his own naturalistic way of looking at life. Although deeply saddened, he didn't feel any misplaced guilt. He and my mother had done everything possible to raise us in the right way, but now we were all adults and had to make our own life choices, and be responsible for them.

My mother couldn't seem to recover from the shock; she became more emotional and would often say, "Her behavior is going to end up sending me to the crazy house." Gradually, her self-fulfilling prophecy came true, and she became bedridden. The doctors could provide no effective treatment, because her symptoms were obviously psychosomatic.

Since my plans for a sports career had ended, I had been working in the grocery business following high school, and had managed to save some money. This crisis in the family led me to take some time off, in order to search for explanations and answers for what had happened. During this period, I got back into my art, which served as a creative escape from all the problems. I enrolled in some art classes at nearby Ventura College, and also began an intense practice of spiritual introspection and prayer. One day, while I was immersed in one of these deeply meditative states, I had what I later learned was an out-of-body-experience, which is recognized in the field of parapsychology as an OBE.

At the time, I had no idea of what was happening, as my awareness just seemed to rise out of my physical body. I was afraid, and thought to myself, "Am I going crazy, too?"

It just so happened that when I was looking through the Ventura College Adult Education schedule, I saw that a lecturer named Dr. Benito Reyes, who had been a famous educator in the Philippines, was starting a course on the evidence for out-of-body experiences. The course description seemed to exactly match my own experience, and was a perfect way for me to reconcile and integrate my experience. I also started to attend some courses and lectures at a small private university which Dr. Reyes had started in the neighboring town of Ojai, and this expanded my knowledge of the spiritual realms of existence even further.

These new insights provided me with a way of helping my mother get out of the guilt trip that had paralyzed her life, and which the teachings of her traditional church had only reinforced. These insights also helped us all come to terms with the tragedies that occurred in the family. Sadly, my sister didn't change her lifestyle, and eventually died of a heroin overdose.

Further upset to the family was caused when the son of another sister was hit by a motorcycle, sustaining permanent injuries that required the kind of care his mother was unable to provide. But this latest heartbreak provided my mother with a new lease on life; she started to take care of her grandson, and it gave her an important reason to carry on living.

I went back to work, and became a meat-cutter in a large grocery chain. Things were going well. I was enjoying life, but one day, I was in the meat cooler at work, and found myself breaking into a sweat. I felt as though it were a boiling hot summer's day, even though the temperature in the cooler registered well below 60 degrees. Then I started to feel nauseous, and knew I had to get to the break room to lie down. I called out to one of my co-workers, saying, "Tell the supervisor that I need help. I'm feeling really bad." The supervisor didn't take the message seriously, but luckily my colleague did, and said, "Hold on, I'm going to call an ambulance."

As I was being driven to the local hospital, I started convulsing. They got me partially stabilized, and immediately arranged for a helicopter to fly me to a larger facility in Thousand Oaks, where they could perform serious emergency heart surgery. As the medical teams were doing their utmost to save my life, I found myself leaving my body and temporarily dying into the most powerful presence of compassion. I felt myself cradled as a newborn child, and underwent the sensation of being submerged into a vast "knowing." Even though I still experienced my own separate consciousness, I was certain that if I could go a little further into this realm of existence that "we" would merge. Every part of me was longing to do just that, but somehow I knew that I had to return to my body and my unfinished life. There was so much I needed to do, especially now that I had real knowledge of this infinite love that not only awaited us, but makes up our very essence.

When I came around after the operation, my family members surrounded the bedside. The doctor told me, "You're the luckiest man alive, because you flatlined twice during the operation, and we thought we'd lost you — but the operation has been a success."

I thought to myself, "If you knew where I had been, you'd really know how lucky I am."

I tried to explain about my experience, but no one understood. The NDE concept was still relatively new, and my doctors and family put my alleged experiences down to the effects of the anesthesia.

Although the operation had saved my life, my heart had been damaged, and that was something I was just going to have to get used to. It also meant that I had to take early retirement. In my spare time, I tried to express my NDE in my artwork.

As I mused over my experience, I realized that there were still certain aspects of it that I needed to get clarification on. Fortunately, I found the right person to help me integrate my experience in the form of Bear Watcher, an Apache medicine man, who was originally from the mountains of Arizona.

For the Native American people, the symbol of the bear has long been associated with shamanism, and for certain indigenous cultures, the bear was known as the first great shaman, who was endowed with the power of divination. Through donning the guise or the name of the animal the shaman is connected to a mythical ancestor, and gets in touch with a power that is greater than himself, for the bear represents a messenger of the Gods and symbolizes the continuum of death and rebirth through its own life cycle, as it hibernates during the winter months and re-emerges with the awakening of spring.

Bear Watcher's name not only reminded him to watch his actions, but also to listen and observe his inner nature, learning to live life from the inside out. He formulated a method of teaching which he called "diamond awareness," and it confirmed the insights I had experienced during my NDE. Bear Watcher told me, "Your NDE has been a great spiritual gift. Now you understand that at the heart of everything there is clarity, love, and compassion." As a shaman, Bear Watcher understood about my NDE, for he had experienced this altered state of consciousness many times.

After spending time working with Bear Watcher, I was able to finish a major piece of art which captured the essence of my extraordinary experience and conveyed its spiritual dimension. I began to think that my paintings might serve to help others understand and reconnect with our journey through this life and into the afterlife.

I became interested in relating to children in this respect, and started to be invited to give talks and show my art to kids in primary school. The art I have produced since my NDE has provided a wonderful "calling card" to show them the true meaning of our lives, and I have discovered that young people respond in a really positive way. They still have the potential to live in their imaginations, and can readily understand that life is a creative experience and needs to be lived positively, in that awareness. Some of the kids I meet come from poor families, or have often had severe hardships to overcome. They definitely need to hear something which can help to inspire them. In my own way, I'm a witness for the everyday person that there is another dimension: you can label it any way you want, but I think Heaven is a good word. Or you can simply translate it to mean another form of consciousness.

Since my NDE, my artistic ability has changed and I have experienced many more visions of altered states of consciousness. Lately, I've really been working on developing my computer skills, and have been able to create many new and exciting images. Recently, a new gymnasium was built at Isbell Elementary, and former students of John Divine lobbied to have it named in his honor. A friend remembered that I had been painting Mr. Divine's portrait, and asked me to become involved in the project. I happily agreed. In my talk to the Santa Paula City Council, I told of all the lives this wonderful teacher had enriched through the thirty-year span of his career. I also volunteered to show my art in classes at the school while discussing his philosophies, as a continuation of his work. The new building is now called the John Divine gym, and my portrait of him talking with three students is now nearly finished. It will be placed in the new gym as a reminder of how much positive difference in people's lives one person can make.

Life has become living in the present moment, which is a joyous experience. I still live in Santa Paula, but now reside in a senior mobile home park, and I love it. Even though my youth was fraught with serious illness and seemed stilted at the time, I have managed to recapture some of that youthful imagination and loving playfulness that I believed had eluded me.

* * * * *

Richie's NDE gave him a new awareness of the preciousness of life and a certainty that consciousness exists after death of the physical body. He experienced connection to a higher source and glimpsed the reality of an afterlife, where infinite love awaits us all at the end of earthly existence. When he returned from this threshold, Richie discovered that his experience in the Light had made it possible for him to expand and express his unique creative talent. Through his art work, he depicts the spiritual dimension of life that operates outside of time, space and logic, as witnessed during his NDE. He now actively uses this medium to help young people share his profound insights and recapture the ability to recognize that we are all interconnected, and that our child-like selves are the parts of us that are often closest to God or a higher power. Richie illustrates how these aspects of our being can be readily accessed and continue to reside deep within us.

LARRY'S STORY

Man – a being in search of meaning
Plato

Larry Hagman experienced life in a "golden prison." He had acquired all the trappings of a successful actor, and was surrounded by a loving and supportive family, but he was troubled. He needed to know the true meaning of life. His psychotherapist recognized this as being an obstacle in Larry's quest to free himself from his self-imposed lock-up, and suggested LSD as a key to expanding his limited consciousness. Larry's experiment was carefully and even reverently arranged with the help of a friend who knew the proper parameters. Through his NDE-like experience, he discovered that Love was the answer to his existential question.

Larry Hagman lives in the small, southern California town of Ojai, which is renowned for its serenity and for surroundings of exquisite beauty. In late 2001, Hagman appeared on the Larry King show, and mentioned having had a near-death experience. Some time later, he was doing a book signing for his recent autobiography, *Hello Darlin',* at the local bookstore. Quite a crowd had gathered on a large patio behind the store, with Larry jovially signing away. He is an open and engaging man, who seems much more like Major Nelson (the character he portrayed in the television series *I dream of Jeanie*) than the power-hungry and scheming J.R. Ewing (from *Dallas*). There is a definite expansive Texan persona about Larry, and he comes across as genuine and friendly.

Larry agreed to discuss his NDE in relation to how it affects the practice of conscious living and dying. "Give me a call," he said, believing in the importance of the project. Taking a $10,000 bill from the stack next to him, he added his phone number and handed it over.

On the reverse side of the bill, in small letters, is the declaration: "This note isn't worth the paper it's printed on." Also included is a reminder to make arrangements to donate our organs upon physical death: "This is printed on recycled paper. Why not recycle yourself? To receive an organ donor card, please call 800-622-9010." An organ recipient himself, Larry underwent a liver transplant that saved his life. As Honorary Chairman of the National Kidney Foundation — a non-profit organization that deals with all aspects of organ transplantation — Larry now works diligently to motivate donors to become "Good Samaritans" and enable others to share the gift of a second chance at life. There are over 89,000 people awaiting such life-saving operations, and the list grows every month. Ten percent of these patients are under eighteen years of age. Every day, seventeen people die because there is no suitable donor.

Home for Larry is his mountain estate in Upper Ojai, named, "Heaven." Looking out over the magnificent panorama that extends all the way to the distant ocean, it is easy to understand why he and his wife picked such an appropriate name. As we entered his home, he stopped to admire the beauty and delicate fragrance from a vase of red roses in the hallway, and his immediate sensitivity to and appreciation of the natural world was obvious.

Larry has undergone two experiences that contain classic NDE elements, but they also share similarities with threshold-of-death experiences more commonly known as death-bed visions. As mentioned earlier, these occur when a person is either approaching death, or is just about to die, and a psychic sensitivity is activated that enables glimpses of the afterlife to manifest into conscious awareness.

* * * * *

Larry

After experiencing withdrawal symptoms related to the use of a prescribed medication and giving up tobacco, Larry sought counseling. One day his therapist gave him a copy of *The Joyous Cosmology*, a book by Alan Watts that describes alternative ways to view perception, consciousness, and spirituality. From that point on, Larry became curious and interested in studying alternative ways of thinking.

In *Hello Darlin'*, Larry describes how during a therapy session, he had the following insight: "I didn't have anything to complain about. Not anything real."

"Exactly," his therapist confirmed. "You've been coming here for a couple of years, and we could be in therapy for as long as you want. But you're troubled by the same things as you were when you came here. As I told you then, you're in a golden prison. But life is not so bad, is it? You don't need therapy as much as a lot of other people. I know what you should do. You should drop some acid."

Larry thought about this option, and says, "The idea of trying LSD lodged in my brain and wouldn't go away. I thought that maybe it would offer a chance of finally getting to know myself better. I procured some pure LSD from a friend and decided that for my initial journey, I would be wise to try it with someone who knew the ropes and would act as my guide.

I fasted for a couple of days, as directed, and then swallowed a tablet and sat back and waited for something to happen. Without any warning, I felt a buzz just below my navel. Suddenly, the entrance to a cave appeared across the room from me — it was guarded by two octopus-like creatures with long writhing tentacles. There were also two other entities that looked like feathery lions. Turning my head, I saw my grandmother, who'd died when I was twelve. She was to my left, hovering about eight feet above me. She sat in the same position I was in, and wore the same kind of robe. She didn't speak, but simply looked at me with a wonderful comforting smile, and told me not to worry.

"All of this is a natural thing," she said. "You're at the gate of all new experiences. The guards at the gate are to keep you from entering. But don't worry about it. If something tries to pull you, don't resist. Go with it. If you feel pushed, don't fight it. Just go with the flow."

All of a sudden, I understood what was happening, and thought about some of the passages I'd read in *The Joyous Cosmology*, and *The Tibetan Book of the Dead* — they all related basically the same thing that my Grandma had just communicated.

I headed for the cave. As soon as I got to the entrance, BOOM, I was sucked inside and down a tunnel at incredible speed. At the end, I saw a light. Coming out of the tunnel, I was in a place where I was surrounded by bright and diffused lights, and saw a person who called out to me. The person didn't talk, but without speaking somehow let me know, "This is a glimpse of where you have been, where you're going, where you are all the time."

It was too much for me to comprehend. The Being seemed to understand that I was having trouble making sense of it all, and communicated: "You don't have to go any further. Having seen this is enough for now."

At that point, I was pulled back through the tunnel. The guards at the gate were asleep. I looked around for my grandmother. She was gone. I wanted to thank her for taking me to the entrance.

Then I got an orange from the kitchen. When I tried to open it, I saw its cellular structure pulsate. It looked to me like the actual cells were vibrating between life and death. It all seemed perfectly natural. I was studying the orange while standing in front of a mirror. When I looked up and saw my face — it was doing the same thing. The cells were pulsating. Some were dying and some were in the process of being reborn. It was an intricate picture. Every molecule was in constant motion. I stared at my face for some considerable time, but after a while, I realized I was a continuous flow of energy. I was part of everything, and everything was part of me. Everything was living, dying, and being reborn.

My guide, who had not taken LSD, drove me around Beverley Hills. Equipped with a sixteen-millimeter camera, I zoomed in on plants, flowers and people. Their cells were also pulsating and changing shape. Besides self-insight, I also saw deeply into people's emotions, and how they were expressed through body and facial language.

The altered state of consciousness was extremely unsettling, but just about the best thing that ever happened to me. It changed my way of looking at people. More than anything else the insights changed my way of looking at life and death.

We don't disappear when we "die." We become part of a curtain of energy. In almost every religion I know about, they say, "As it was in the beginning, is now, and ever shall be." I had an understanding that God is consciousness. It was so clear. The LSD experience took the fear of death from me, the fear of manmade heaven and hell. With that out of the way, I quit worrying.

Toward the end of his book, Larry relates the next segment of his journey into a higher dimension of consciousness. He was in an intensive care unit, following his liver transplant operation. Although heavily medicated, he was conscious enough to think of some mantras and meditated on his favorite image: a field of brightly colored yellow mustard flowers that had a red rose in the middle. He focused on what he calls his "celestial song." "Everyone has their own unique song," he noted, "an inner melody that fuses us to the deep, modulating, harmonious hum of the celestial orchestra that's the collective energy of everything that's ever lived and ever going to live. It's our life force. The power of the universe."

Shamans discover their sacred songs during their vision journeys, and Larry experienced his own vision journey through meditating on his song. He turned his isolation in the ICU into a context similar to the isolation of a shamanic journey or vision quest, where a ceremonial, meditative practice is enacted. "The days I spent in ICU meditating on my song gave me a feeling that was ecstatically happy and so familiar — and it confirmed what I'd always suspected: every one of us living creatures is part of a collective energy that is also ecstatically happy and familiar. The culmination of that energy is love. It's with us now, it always has been, and it always will be. Every one of us has this awareness. We know it. The problem is, we bury it under so much apprehension and worry."

As with his LSD experience years before, Larry "glimpsed over the edge of this level into the next, and there was that person again..." The same Being, who had welcomed him into the light as he emerged through the tunnel while under the influence of LSD, greeted him again. But Larry understood that it was "not yet time to cross over." He was also granted a deep insight and understanding: "This was not the end. There were more levels, an infinite number of levels, of existence, each one adding to the hum of the cosmic orchestra, as if we're always spiraling upward until we reach a state of atomic bliss..."

It occurred to Larry that every religion he knew of had tried to figure out the meaning of life, and had essentially reached the same conclusion — the meaning of life is Love. His resulting philosophy following his second NDE-like vision is:

> "Don't worry
> Be Happy
> Feel Good"

* * * * *

Visiting Larry at his mountain estate provided a chance to ask him personally what he had learned from the life-enhancing impact usually associated with these powerful events, in which mythological elements were natural components of his experience. Like Dante's Beatrice, his guide to higher realms was a beloved female figure – his grandmother. Her comforting presence helped him adjust and feel at home in the cosmos. Larry focused on the intrinsic value of relationships and leading a life of service, and explains how his LSD experiment and NDE-like experience had made him so much more aware and appreciative of everything about life and how we live it. Our interconnectedness continues to be so apparent, and this has made him more compassionate. He and his wife have involved themselves in many community service projects of various kinds, and he chooses to aid causes that he not only believes in, but which also interest him and give something back in a kind of symbiotic energy exchange. The "crossing over," altered state of consciousness experiences have given him a belief that life continues and that love abounds, with its feelings of ecstasy and deep bliss.

After an illuminating conversation, our visit concluded in the late afternoon. As we walked with Larry down the long hallway to the door, the low midwinter sun was coming in through the west-facing windows, sending shafts of soft light to flood across the beautiful floor tiles. Larry paused, and motioned us to stop and enjoy this vision for a moment. It was indeed a glorious sight — one that reflected the rhythms and beauty of the natural world that are often missed, as we hurry by without giving them a second glance.

DYING TO EXPERIENCE LIFE

*All men's souls are immortal, but the souls of the righteous
are immortal and divine*
Socrates

Plato's dying words and final instructions to his disciples are just as relevant in modern-day society as they were in his time, for they imply that the moment of death and its quality is dependent upon the way we live our lives, and where our consciousness has been placed. We need a philosophy of life that ultimately becomes a practice for the act and art of living and dying well, and making our transition into the eternal continuum of consciousness.

Plato's dialogue about justice in society and within the individual resonates with the Indian concept of Dharma or right conduct, which is illuminated in the *Bhagavad-Gita.* This sacred text opens on the battle-field, as Prince Arjuna becomes full of doubt about fulfilling his duty as a warrior when confronted by a just battle against his own family members. In his anguish, he turns to Sri Krishna, an avatar of Sri Vishnu who is acting as his charioteer, and asks him for guidance. Krishna reminds Arjuna of his obligations, and advises him that the soul is immortal and that death on the battlefield would only mean shedding the physical body. He explains that true enlightenment necessitates relinquishing the false sense of self that resonates with the illusion of mortality, in order to gain knowledge of the existence of the true self which is the immortal life of the soul or atman. So that he may appreciate his divine nature, Krishna grants Arjuna the ability to temporarily view his Divine immortal form.

In this dialogue, the metaphor of the "battle" describes the constant struggle and complexity of the human ego that obscures the fact that the spirit of Krishna is alive within all of us, and represents the inner divinity of the human being that lies at our core. The *Bhagavad-Gita* emphasizes that death is part of the cycle of death and resurrection, and the text focuses on the way in which a person should live their life, in accordance with these divine principles.

Near the end of the debate which closes the *Republic*, Socrates has also recounted the various rewards which a just person may expect in his or her lifetime "in addition to those other blessings which come simply from being just." He goes on to relate that these "are as nothing, in number or greatness, when compared with the recompense awaiting the just and the unjust after death."

This final summing up is the finale to the central thesis of the *Republic* what justice is, in the ultimate sense in the word. It is the performance of one's duties according to one's abilities and situation in life. This right conduct must occur within the highest good of the whole society. And what constitutes the highest good? Only a true philosopher such as Socrates may answer that question, and he does so by illustrating that a true doctor, sea captain, or shepherd must act in a responsible way, having the interests of patients, ship and crew, or flock of animals, at the heart of his actions. For Socrates, his dialogue on justice was based on relating actual events. When he was asked to explain what he meant, he simply recounted many instances in which this quality of being was illustrated. His conversations captured the essence of a meaning that is an eternal presence through example.

Socrates pointed out that justice in the form of recompense will be awarded to these people in various ways throughout their lives, both in this world and the next. This certainly can include material success, but their actions cannot be contingent on gaining power or money, for then they would not be acting in an authentic manner. Socrates demonstrates that justice is a state in which each individual contributes to the well-being of the whole of society, in the context of the "good" which philosophers know, love, and serve.

Plato concludes the *Republic* with a beautiful description of the process:

And so, Glaucon, his story wasn't lost but preserved, and it would save us, if we were persuaded by it, for then we would make a good crossing of the River of Forgetfulness, and our souls wouldn't be defiled. But if we are persuaded by me, we'll believe that the soul is immortal and able to endure every evil and every good and we'll always hold to the upward path, practicing justice with reason in every way. That way we'll be friends with the Gods while we remain here on earth and afterwards – like victors in the games who go round collecting their prizes – we'll receive our rewards. Hence, both in this life and on the thousand-year journey we've described, we'll do well and be happy.

If we are to behave consciously, mindful of the essential values in this life and our dying process, then we need to activate and honor our conscience and begin to embrace the *Buddhi* faculty of illumined inner knowing, which is determined in both the spiritual traditions of India and the Greek wisdom of Socrates. These principles can guide our thoughts, actions, and interactions throughout this world and the next, and constitute the true consolation of philosophy — the Love of Wisdom, the Wisdom of Love, and the art of living and dying well.

Less than a hundred years ago, it was impossible to escape or deny the reality of death, for epidemics of child-hood diseases and limited medical knowledge resulted in death and dying as being a part of everyday life. In contemporary Western cultures, advancements in health care and a longer life span have resulted in society adopting the concept of ignoring death, the dying and the bereaved, in order to somehow forget that death is an integral part of life. This approach leads to fear and alienation from the ultimate reality of existence, and leaves us traumatized and feeling alone, when the inescapability of death touches our lives. However, a deeper understanding of the enormity and inevitability of death, which may claim those of any age or circumstances, can result in a positively transformative, life-affirming experience. For as the great poet Rilke reminds us:

Death is the *side of life* that is turned away from us: we must try to achieve the fullest consciousness of our existence, which is at home in *the two unseperated realms, inexhaustibly nourished by both...there is neither a here nor a beyond, but the great unity,* in which those creatures that surpass us, the 'angels', are at home.

Contemplating the death of others provides the opportunity to deconstruct the myth built up with the temporary attributes of "self," which will eventually perish at death. The human being is the only animal that understands the concept of physical death and the immortality of the soul and, as Sathya Sai Baba, the renowned spiritual leader, states:

Man alone has the strange thirst after the nectar that confers immortality. That is his special task, his special quest, the quest for the truth that emancipates.

The individual who has been touched by the profoundness of death, either through an NDE, or through observing or participating in another's dying process, can be expanded into an awareness of life being lived beyond the constriction of the small or ego-based self. The experience can shake the foundations of preconceived ideas about life, and awaken a commitment to be of service. Often this is performed in a way that is selfless.

With this new appreciation of the truth, the profound insights lead to an understanding of the connectedness of all beings and the realization that through service to others, we are also serving ourselves and facilitating a process of allowing the heart to open, thus enabling love to flow more freely. It is then possible to live in a more selfless manner, and to activate the expansive nature that lies at the core of our being. As the great Indian spiritual leader, Mahatma Gandhi, once said, "The best way to find yourself is to lose yourself in the service of others."

Rather than trying to ignore or escape from the reality of physical death, one acknowledges its inescapable inevitability, and not only comes to terms with it, but uses it as a reminder of how precious life is, and of the chance it offers for learning how to be most authentically human. The Buddhist scriptures illustrate this teaching in the story of a woman who came from a poor family, and was looked upon with contempt by her husband's relatives. When she gave birth to a son, their disdain changed to respect. However, a few years later, the son died, and the woman became distraught with grief. She searched everywhere for a cure that would bring her dead son back to life, but could find none. In her despair, she visited the Buddha, to see if he could help her. The Buddha told her to go back to her community and collect a mustard seed from a household where there had been no death. The woman searched for days, believing that if she could fulfill the Buddha's request, her son would be returned to her. But she eventually returned to the Buddha empty-handed, and realized that there was no cure for death; it was an irrevocable part of life that everyone had to experience. However, she was cured of her grief, and decided to become a disciple of the Buddha.

As he lay on his deathbed, the Buddha reminded his followers of the impermanence of life, and of how all things would eventually decay and perish. He encouraged people to accept death as a motivating force that provides a foundation for living life consciously and well. Actively engaging with a dying person, or being deeply touched by the death of our fellow pilgrims through the voyage of life, teaches us to value and make the most of a temporary visit to the planet Earth; this then becomes the practice of conscious living and dying.

A sense of empathy can result from these deep reflections, resulting in the ability to have compassion for others. The Dalai Lama considers compassion to be the supreme emotion, and the most precious quality the human being can possess. In *Compassion and Bodhicitta,* he states:

Every human being has the same potential for compassion; the only question is whether we really take any care of that potential, and develop and implement it in our daily life. My hope is that more and more people will realize the value of compassion, and so follow the path of altruism. As for myself since I became a Buddhist monk, that has been my real destiny – for usually I think of myself as just one simple Buddhist monk, no more and no less.

The word *compassion* is derived from a Sanskrit word that means *the ability to form an unconditional relationship with one's self.* In the Buddhist teachings, the deity, Avalokiteshvara, embodies compassion, and is known as "The Lord who regards the cries of the world." Human suffering stems from the perception of an ego-based consciousness, and this perception arises from ignorance. Compassion requires the ability to discriminate, to see the truth of how things really are and let go of our illusions. The resulting wisdom gained in this process enables one to see that true compassion is not demonstrated through pity for our fellow human beings, but through recognizing the fact that we are all connected and seeking happiness.

The Vietnamese monk, Thich Nhat Hanh, emphasizes "transformational practice" as the way to access compassion for ourselves and others. In *A Dialogue of Reconciliation*, he teaches that "the first step to peacemaking and compassionate action is watering the seeds of peace and uprooting the seeds of war in your own heart."

Compassion requires a genuine desire to release people from their suffering, with no hidden motives or selfish desires that result from an attachment to the outcome of our actions. Acts of loving kindness to others provide a means of demonstrating compassion and becoming aware of: the children who have no shoes, the homeless who live on the fringe of society, those fighting terminal illness, the plight of people in countries ravished by war, and the destruction of the planet.

Through understanding the power of good intention, it is possible see how thoughts, actions and words — both positive and negative — travel and touch others. Thinking ill of another can harm them, and ultimately results in harm to ourselves. But positive intentions benefit those around us, and lead to the reaping of personal rewards in which former values are relinquished. Instead of accumulating material possessions for personal gain; one starts to reach out and give to others, and becomes liberated from self-absorbed ways of moving through the world.

For many who are seeking a sense of meaning in their lives, interacting with someone in the dying process serves as a catalyst to dive into the very essence of the inner being, and to experience a profound spiritual transformation. For those close to death are in an altered state of consciousness, and choosing to accompany them on part of their journey enables the heart to open up to compassion. Through focusing in the present moment and peeling off the layers of fear and tension that are a form of spiritual dormancy, it is possible to realize our highest potential as human beings.

The dying process and its aftermath can also facilitate a time of reconciliation, in which bitter rifts and estrangements are healed. This can enable individuals to move forward in a state of wisdom and grace, and to reconnect with an expanded awareness that illuminates a sense of destiny and purpose. For death engages a psychic, numinous energy that shifts preconceived perceptions of the essential meaning of life.

Every interaction with death and dying involves entering the underworld of painful grief and suffering, but each also provides the opportunity to emerge from the experience with a sense of awe, and greater insight into the mystery of creation. Death teaches us that the preciousness of life must be lived with a sense of purpose and meaning, and as a celebration of our existence. Often, these philosophical reflections instill the urge and inspiration to help and serve others as we discover the larger concept, in which it is possible to put into practice these newfound truths that have value beyond death. For the dying process is a ritual, and serves as an initiation into the understanding of what it really means to live.

The Golden Rule embraces a fundamental tenet at the heart of all religions: "treat others as you wish them to treat you." Practicing this set of principles often becomes difficult when life appears to be a battle for survival, rather than an enlightened journey. But there is a constant reminder in all the religious texts, telling us how pointless it is to bow at the altar of the Gods if we do not live life in the context of the well-being of the whole. Sathya Sai Baba illustrates the value and rewards of selfless service in the *Yoga of Action*, saying:

> Cultivate the Divine qualities of love, compassion, humility and reverence towards the earth and all the other elements. You can thus draw upon yourself the grace of God and render your life beneficial and fruitful. More than listening to a hundred lectures or delivering them to others, offering one act of genuine service attracts the grace of God.

The universal principles of selfless service provide a basis for many of the world's religions, including Christianity, Buddhism, and Hinduism. In Eastern philosophies, these values are practiced in bhakti Yoga, which is similarly based on the Christian values of extending charity to all our fellow human beings. In each of these traditions, God is perceived as residing in the hearts of all beings, and serving another is viewed a fundamental practice of devotion.

Native American religious rituals include vision quests, fasting, sweat lodges and the sun dance, and the object of each is to strip away the outer layers of the personality and access the essential being, in order to facilitate communication with the spirit world in a state of humility and receptiveness. These rituals are practiced to gain knowledge from the spirits, who can assist these people to live their lives for the well-being of the entire community.

One might think that a belief in God and the afterlife would be the strongest motivation for selfless service, but that is not always the case. In the book and film *Keys to the Kingdom*, one of the minor characters is a Western medical doctor who professes to be a devout atheist, but who nevertheless behaves like a saint when treating his Chinese patients.

Beyond the Call is a recent film documentary in which producer-director, Adrian Belic, captures on film the heroic efforts of Ed Artis, James Law, and Walt Ratterman, who have formed themselves into a "self styled order" based on the renowned acts of chivalry and deeds of the fabled Templar Knights, who existed for some two-hundred years during the Middle Ages. Knightsbridge International has evolved into a small California-based humanitarian relief organization that has provided millions of dollars worth of food, medicine and shelter to people in the remotest locations of the world, who suffer from the ravages of war and natural disasters.

This trio of middle-aged and unlikely heroes — comprised of an army medic, a cardiologist, and an entrepreneur — has journeyed all over the globe, venturing through Afghanistan, Albania, Cambodia, Chechnya, Kosovo and, most recently, the war torn southern Philippines, bringing relief to poor and desperate people. While controversy exists over what some people deem to be their "Robin Hood" tactics, Artis, Law, and Ratterman have gone into the most dangerous terrain on their missions of mercy. They have handed out cash to Afghan schools, and paid for truck-loads of supplies; and the only important thing, for them, is to make these things happen.

Artis explains that Knightsbridge is not interested in changing people's religious or political beliefs, but concerned instead with making a difference in the lives of these people. Their daring exploits, described as a cross between the work of Mother Teresa and the adventures of Indiana Jones, bring them into daily contact with death and dying caused by famine, disease, landmines, bullets, bombs, and the elements. While shying away from the concept of a spiritual dimension to their work, Artis does concede that when he suffered a heart attack during one of his missions, he felt some kind of profound realization as he hovered between life and death. He comments:

I did not see a blue light. I did not see God or anything like that. But what I saw, what I felt was an incredible clarity, a clear thought. Just like, it's OK, I surrender to my fate. If I die, I die. I did like an instant spread sheet of my whole life, and it was more positive than negative, so it was OK.

But I still got mad at myself for the life I had wasted and the things I had not done. Not things for me, but for others…my wife, my friends, and those who cared for me and the work I was trying to do. I realized that I didn't share enough of my feelings with them, or the thoughts and ideas I had on how we could help more people in so many different ways.

Since then, I have tried to say good things to as many people as possible on a daily basis, and to share all of my thoughts, ideas and methods of doing things with anyone and everyone. I don't want to take this skill to the grave with me. I don't have that right, because the lessons I have learned are to be shared with humanity.

I'm no Saint, but I do hold to the values of being a Knight, and although I've made some enemies, I would do it all over again. Even though my work has cost me my health, I know that just one person can make a difference, and I see that reflected every day in the faces of the people who benefit through the work that our organization implements.

Knightsbridge International is presently involved in developing a project in the north of Niger, where there is currently no medical facility serving the Nomadic People in the region, who are known as the Tuarag and represent 8% of the national population.

Two of the following stories also involve individuals who do not consider themselves to be religious, or even necessarily spiritual. But they too provide examples of people who are sincere in their desire to be of service to the community. Following interactions with the dying process, their subsequent activities place them in the realm of sainted company.

A Year to Live is a program devised by Stephen and Ondrea Levine, who, as part of their spiritual path and life mission, provide guidance and care to the dying. Their valuable work illustrates how a year spent invoking the practice of letting go, and activating an awareness and acceptance of the dying process, is a transformative exercise. The end result is a resolve to be of greater service, and to fully savor every moment of life.

The practice of loving kindness is also a way of reaching out to others, providing an opportunity to give back and reflect gratitude for all the things we have to be grateful for. The effects of a simple act of kindness reverberate like ripples on a pool. As illustrated in Joanne's Story, caring for others can bring immense joy into the lives of both the donors and recipients of such acts, for kindness connects us to one other. Viktor Frankl illustrates this concept poignantly in his book *Man's Search for Meaning*, as he describes how acknowledging another with a simple nod or smile gave that person the will to carry on living in the face of the appalling brutality, inhuman conditions and death that were experienced daily in the Nazi concentration camps. He writes:

The experiences of camp life show that a man does have a choice of actions. There were enough examples, often of a heroic nature, which proved that apathy could be overcome, irritability suppressed. Man can preserve a vestige of spiritual freedom, of independence of mind, even in such terrible conditions of psychic and physical stress.

We who lived in concentration camps can remember the men who walked through the huts comforting others, giving away their last piece of bread... they offer proof that everything can be taken from a man but one thing: the last of the human freedoms – to choose one's attitude in any given set of circumstances.

Interacting with death reflects the reality and significance of life and altruistic love and can also stimulate the creative world of the imagination that remembers something bigger than the "self." Peter's Story demonstrates just how much can be accomplished by one man who has his heart in the right place. His dedication to bring joy into the life of seriously ill children motivated others to join him in his endeavors. Involvement in the dying process is often an invitation to continue the work of the healer, the poet, and the philosopher — who use their creative gifts in the service of humanity.

In the Zen tradition (known as "Chan" in China) there is the concept of the gradual awakening to innate truth or enlightenment, and the concept of sudden awakening. This latter experience is not necessarily confined to Zen, but can happen to anyone at any time; the following story of Wilma Melville appears to be of this type. Her experience at the scene of the Oklahoma bombing had such a deep and visceral impact that it awakened an immediate compassionate response. The result was her mission to provide a greater number of rescue dogs to help in any subsequent disasters, and millions saw the result of her efforts televised all around the globe through the grueling rescue mission at the scene of 9/11.

The death of a beloved son during the 9/11 terror attacks prompted his parents, Sally and Donald, to contribute to the rebuilding of Afghanistan, which was destroyed by senseless acts of war. This spontaneous and huge leap of faith opened the door to healing, and the rebuilding of a school that was desperately needed in the community.

As demonstrated in all of these next stories, it is impossible to avoid the death of the physical body, but one can leave the memory of a life well-lived to those left behind, planting a seed for future generations to tend and cultivate.

Many of the world's problems and injustices are a result of meaningless acts of self-gratification, which result in an inability to look beyond the self and reach out to one's fellow human beings and to all life forms that inhabit and share the planet Earth. Engagement with death provides a stark reminder of the futility of these actions, by shaking us out of complacency and providing an alternative way of living. Fully engaging with death and dying heralds the opportunity to draw from the well of the inner being, and find the jewels of love and compassion. Through the acknowledgement of physical death and the dying process, the individual becomes free to live life more fully, and to experience the boundless unconditional love and beauty that constantly surrounds us.

JOANNE'S STORY

Be kind, for everyone you meet is fighting a harder battle
Plato

Joanne Cacciatore's daughter, Cheyenne, brought the two miracles of our existence – birth and death – so close together that you could be forgiven for thinking that she'd never truly lived. But she did live. In fact she had a glorious life, and illustrated that a soul could enter this earthly existence for the briefest of time, and yet send shockwaves throughout the world for years afterwards.

Joanne found the courage to let her emotional tide of grief and anguish run its course, and emerged from the experience profoundly changed, spiritually awakened, and ready to listen to the promptings of her soul.

Ominous billowing clouds have begun to form in the sky over Phoenix. A forty-mile-an-hour gale is picking up momentum, filling the air with course, swirling sand. Joanne is a warm and vibrant woman, who appears to be totally unfazed by the sound of the wind tearing through the neighborhood. She makes some tea, and then sits on the floor of her comfortable living room to tell her story.

* * * * *

Joanne

The turning point in my life happened eight years ago, at the beginning of Arizona's monsoon season. I was in the hospital, about to give birth to my fourth child, Cheyenne. Everything was ready: her nursery had been decorated, new clothes had been placed in her baby chest of drawers, and my mother had just finished knitting a warm blanket for her. Everybody was excited, especially my other children, who loved to see their sister's tiny ultrasound shadow kicking up a storm on the monitor. During my pregnancy, I had felt so in awe of the miracle of having this new life forming inside me, as I felt her moving her little arms and legs about.

"Twenty minutes to go," I thought, "Maybe less, and then Cheyenne will be in my arms".

Then things started to go wrong. I sensed a subtle change in the mood of the doctors, and I saw them exchange furtive glances. There was an awkward silence in the room, the sort that heralds bad news. I could feel myself beginning to panic.

A doctor said, "We can't detect a heartbeat, Joanne".

My physical pain instantly gave way to emotional agony; it was so great that I could only escape it by drifting out of my body. I kept on thinking: "This can't be happening. Cheyenne will be alive, I know it".

But I was wrong. When she was born, she did not gasp or cry and gulp in her first breath. Except for the sound of the monsoon rains still hammering against the windows, there was just an eerie silence, as though a thick fog had descended over the room. It all felt so surreal.

The doctor asked me if I wanted to hold her. I sat up and gathered her in my arms. I was overcome with a mixture of sadness and joy. She was perfect — absolutely gorgeous, with flawless skin and ebony hair. She looked like she was merely sleeping. I dressed her, took pictures, kissed her, caressed her, and stroked her still-warm cheeks. Then after a while, her skin began to blister, and the nurses urged me to let them take her to the morgue.

When they opened the door to take her away, I could hear all the other babies on the maternity ward crying. It was unreal. I was overwhelmed with grief, and yet there was no one in the hospital able to give me the comfort or help that I needed. I realized I had to get out of the place. Just two hours after Cheyenne was born, I walked out of the hospital carrying a little plastic teddy bear under my arm, and started a downwards spiral into Hades.

At Cheyenne's funeral, there was a blanket of flowers, and a line of black limousines. As the minister conducted the service, the tiny casket was lowered into the earth. "Another kind of womb," I thought, as the earth was shoveled over her. Cheyenne was gone.

I wrote in my journal that evening:

Pink, white and blue were my choices — not for pretty dresses, but for your casket. We all dreamed of your future — your first day in kindergarten, your college graduation, your wedding day; we even imagined your first bite of a messy, ripe peach. We thought of so many things, but we never imagined your life would end before it had begun.

Scarcely a month had passed before people were urging me to move on with my life. They wanted me to be the person I was before, gregarious and fun-loving. All the pressure to return to normal made it far worse for me. In my grief, I felt isolated from my family and friends. My only source of comfort was my three-year-old daughter. She was wise beyond her years, and would wrap her arms around me and say, "Mommy, it's all right to cry; babies shouldn't die."

Gradually, I came to the understanding that grief is as personal to each individual as a fingerprint. Everyone has to experience it in their own way, if they are to survive. Grief has no timetable, and it can't be washed away with platitudes. The loss is immense, painful beyond description, and yet you have to let it work through your complete being by experiencing it fully, with as many tears as you need to shed. At the end of the process, the pain will dull, and you will move on, but you will never forget.

After Cheyenne's death, I had to fight to stay alive and remain sane. One night I was sitting in the closet with my knees to my chest, rocking myself back and forth, and I realized for the first time that I wouldn't make it unless I got help. I thumbed through the yellow pages and called five non-profit groups, but every number had been disconnected.

The sixth and last number I tried was that of the Compassionate

Friends. An answering machine picked up, and I thought, "Thank God! Finally there is someone I can reach out to." I was so overcome by emotion that I could barely speak. The next day a volunteer called me back, and from that point on, I was no longer alone.

The Compassionate Friends brought me into contact with other grieving parents, and that helped me a lot. This was in sharp contrast to the hospital, which pretty much abandoned me. No social worker had visited, no pastor had offered solace and comfort, and no doctor or nurse had sat on the bed and shared my grief with me. Once I had left the hospital there was no follow-up, and there was no number for me to call in case I needed help. They knew how to take care of me physically, but they had no clue about caring for me emotionally or spiritually.

I felt something had to be done to help others in similar situations, so I started doing research. I became drawn to the work of Elisabeth Kubler-Ross, a Swiss physician and psychiatrist who was a pioneer in the field of death and dying. Her book *On Children and Death* contained universal truths that gave me the light of hope during the darkest time of my life. A once-extinguished flame flickered in my heart, and Elisabeth's teachings encouraged me to take action, as I put together a workshop that trained professionals to provide appropriate support for bereaved parents. I outlined all the things you need to say and do; the importance of ritual and how to include your children in the death experience to help them deal with their own feelings of loss.

After some initial resistance, the hospitals were surprisingly receptive. They allowed me to work alongside their staff, and subsequently started to refer families to me. It was then that I founded MISS, Mothers in Sympathy and Support, which has now grown into an international nonprofit organization that provides aid, support and advocacy for grieving families after a young child dies. Today, we have more than seventy chapters and tens of thousands of members all over the world. More than 120,000 children die each year in the United States, and 80% of them have not reached their first birthday. It's our philosophy that no one should experience the death of a child alone, and we do everything we can to ensure that the medical community provides resources for families who need both support and guidance. We are committed to honoring the memory of the children who lived, who died, and who continue — even in death — to matter.

It wasn't at all like me to become socially active. Before Cheyenne's birth, I saw life in a small, inward-looking way. I had blinders on, and didn't notice the important things — like children who don't have shoes, or old people struggling to open a door. But Cheyenne's birth and death blew me apart, and when the pieces fell back into place, I emerged as a different person. I discovered a purpose to my life, which began to absorb me. People would say, "You're doing such wonderful work," and I'd think, "You don't understand; this is not a choice. There is a force inside me that compels me to do what I do."

Christmas came. I was preparing for the holidays with my children, and I was thinking, "What am I going to do with the Christmas money that I would have spent on Cheyenne?" I knew that I wanted to so something altruistic with it, so I went out shopping and bought six little girl presents and six little boy presents, even though I had no idea of what I was going to do with them. I went to the hospital, but all the children had been discharged for the holiday. The registrar directed me to the Lincoln Learning Center, which provides child-care for lower income families. "The kids there don't get a lot for Christmas," she said, "Try them."

It was truly a miracle, for there were exactly six boys and six girls there that day. I watched through the window as they ripped open the gifts, and I cried with joy, feeling as though my heart had ripped open too. And then this sense of calm descended over me. It was a wonderful feeling of peace. I realized that I had stumbled across an important part of my healing — looking outwards, and doing things to help others.

I began to look for opportunities to be of service to people who needed help, but I didn't want to put myself in the spotlight. On one occasion, I was in a shoe store and I overheard a family talking about which of their four children should have new shoes. They couldn't afford new ones for all of them, but I could see that they all were in need of them. I wanted to help, so I went to the store manager and gave him some money, and said, "Make sure all the children have new shoes and please give them this note." On a piece of paper I'd written, *"In loving memory of my daughter."*

Driving home, I felt as if a huge weight had been lifted from my heart. It was like receiving medicine from heaven. I understood for the first time the blessing of sharing with others anonymously. I felt that other grieving parents would want to experience this too, and so I designed a card that they could use to accompany a gift or service. It read:

This Random Act of Kindness
Done in Loving Memory
Of our Beautiful Child

_____

(Name of child)

I called this the *Kindness Project*. Since its inception nine years ago, we've sold over 700,000 cards in loving memory of children, parents, friends and partners. This kind of action is a legacy that transcends the painful experience of physical death. When bereaved parents are ready, it gives them an opportunity to be able to give back in this way. Once they can focus their attention on others, a process of deep healing is initiated. It's a law; it's more real than the law of gravity. The recipients are helped a lot too, and not just materially. We don't ever believe that our children can die, but when we receive a card that says, *In Loving Memory of our Child,* it makes us stop and reflect. Children come into our lives as a miraculous gift, and sometimes we need to be reminded to express our gratitude.

On the MISS website, there's a Kindness Project Forum Board, where benefactors and recipients can tell their stories. One lady wrote:

> I am a waitress at a Cracker Barrel restaurant in a rural town. I have
> been sad and stressed dealing with a recent divorce. Today, I waited
> on a table with a very nice, attractive couple. When they finished their
> meal, they left an incredibly generous tip wrapped around one of your
> Kindness Cards. I discovered it after they'd left the restaurant. When
> I read the card I went into the back room and cried. I thought about
> my own daughter and how I would feel if she died. When I got home
> from work, I called her to tell her how much I loved her. I realized that
> my life is blessed after all.

I'd never been a political activist, but Cheyenne changed that too. At the
time of her death, Arizona law required parents to obtain a death
certificate and bury a stillborn child, but they were denied a birth
certificate. I found this to be a sad and painful injustice.

The state required an official document to say that the mother gave
death, but wouldn't provide a document that said she gave life. I wasn't
alone in finding this hard. Many bereaved parents I knew felt the same
way. The birth certificates for stillborns are an important form of ritual
that indicates public acknowledgement for families coming to terms with
what has happened. People who don't understand this don't appreciate the
incredible pain that stems from a stillbirth. They presume that the trauma
is small compared with losing a three-year-old. The question I ask them
is: "If God came down into the delivery room, and said, "I'm going to
take your child. Shall I do it now, or when she is a three-year-old?' What
would you say? If you replied, "Take her now," would the grief and pain
be any less?

So I campaigned to have the law changed. After years of lobbying, I
managed to get legislation passed in the state of Arizona that allowed for
a joint birth/death certificate to be issued for a stillborn. Following a
unanimous vote, Senator Susan Gerard, Chair of the Health Committee,

made the following statement:

> The passage of this bill will give much needed respect to those who have experienced the stillbirth of a child. It may even be the first step towards increased knowledge about the causes of stillbirth. In addition, it makes Arizona the first state in what will hopefully be a national trend towards recognizing the significance of this tragedy. I would like to thank Joanne Cacciatore for her leadership and her efforts and her daughter, Cheyenne Cacciatore, for whom this act is named.

Following this work, my life took another surprising turn. A few years ago, I saw a photo of Elisabeth Kubler-Ross that I wanted to use in one of the MISS Foundation conferences. I emailed the photographer to ask for permission. His name was Ken Ross, but I didn't make any connection between him and Elisabeth. In his reply, he asked for more information about my organization, which I mailed back to him. A few days later, he wrote again and suggested I give Elisabeth a call. He said, "My mother would be very happy to meet you."

I was awestruck. She had been my savior years before, and now I was going to meet her in person. I went over to her house and said, "You have no idea how much your books helped me. They made it possible for me to work through my daughter's death."

I started to spend time with Elisabeth. We would talk about many things, or watch a movie together, and we quickly became close friends. Sometimes, we would just sit in the silence and watch the birds or the setting sun. She was the most genuine person that I have ever met; she could be silly and demanding, sensitive and honest or playful and critical. But she was always authentic. During the course of our friendship, there were times when I wanted to give up this work, disheartened by the never-ending sadness of a child's death. Elisabeth would gently remind me that I hadn't chosen this course; but that it had chosen me — and she would encourage me to continue.

Elisabeth's health had been failing following a series of strokes, and she sometimes talked about what it was going to be like to die. She had no fear of her own physical death; in fact she welcomed the impending transition and was impatient to leave the confines of her struggling body. She had lived a very full life, much of it in service to others, and had completed the work she had been sent here to do. She firmly believed that the moment of death freed the soul to return home to God, and was looking forward it. She was going to be buried in the same cemetery as Cheyenne, and had reserved her spot there around about the time Cheyenne died, years before we met.

She wanted to add a few of her own special words to my story:

Joanne Cacciatore (it's a great name) and I first met when she called me after meeting my son, Ken. She read my books about dying children and their near-death experiences after her own child died. The books and my research brought her peace and that peace brought her to me.

We are sisters now. We've known each other many lifetimes and this explains why we became so close. I always thank her for coming to see me, and she always thanks me for being here.

Joanne shares my knowledge, thoughts and ideas about death, dying and grieving. She does the work of my hands. I want her to keep doing it long after I've gone. I promised her that when I die, I'm going to come back and pinch her tush. She says that she'll love it!

On July 24, 2004, exactly one year before her death, I had a dream that Elisabeth died. In the dream, I was grief-stricken and feeling desperate to have my friend back. She appeared to me, surprised by my sadness. She told me to stop crying, and assured me that she was fine, adding that I shouldn't worry, as she was well aware of my enduring tug-of-war with faith. She added, reassuringly, "I'll see you again one day." When I visited her the next morning, I told her about the dream, and she asked, "Was it a good dream?" I replied hesitatingly, "Well, not really." Then she asked, "Did I die?" "Yes," I said looking down. She assured me that when she made her transition, she could help me more with my work from the other side than she could here. I walked away from our conversation knowing that when the time came, it would be very hard to say goodbye. But I knew she would never *really* leave any of us, and that her work would never end.

A year later, Elisabeth's health took a further turn for the worse, and she made her eagerly awaited transition. I came home the night of Elisabeth's funeral services exhausted. I already missed her so much, and felt grief's grip around my chest. Around 11:00 p.m., I went out onto my front patio, sat in my rocking chair and started talking to Elisabeth in my mind. With tears rolling down my cheeks, I asked her for a very clear sign, something like a shooting star, to confirm she was still around. I didn't really expect anything miraculous, but a few minutes later, I opened my eyes to immediately see a bright shooting star traveling from the east to the west in the sky. I realized at that moment that Elisabeth was doing what she had promised. She is busy guiding and inspiring us all, surrounded by stars amongst the galaxies. I remembered her timeless words, "Dying is nothing to fear. It can be the most wonderful experience of your life. It all depends on how you have lived."

When I reflect on my life, since, Cheyenne's death, I realize that it has been touched by two of the most wonderful human beings who ever lived. One of them walked this earth only briefly. The other graced us with her wisdom and teaching for more than seven decades, soaring beyond the expectations for the life of a single mortal. If an angel had come to me years ago and told me what to expect, I wouldn't have believed it. Of course the truth is an angel did come. Her name was Cheyenne, and she came bearing extraordinary gifts. I had been in a state of spiritual dormancy, and her brief earthly existence made me wake up and start to grow. As a result, she ultimately touched the lives of hundreds of thousands of people. And she did it all without taking a single breath or uttering a single word. I call that a miracle!

* * * * *

Joanne is continuing Elisabeth's work by teaching people how to come to terms with the dying process, and helping them to embrace rather than deny it. Part of this work includes the MISS Foundation and the Elisabeth Kubler-Ross Foundation jointly creating a bereavement and trauma center in Phoenix, Arizona. This center will provide services to those who have lost a loved one, serve as a research center, and bring community nonprofit groups and social agencies together to help. It has a goal of opening "The Elizabeth House" by the end of 2008.

PETER'S STORY

Not life, but good life, is chiefly to be valued
Socrates

If we find the courage to look deeply into the eyes of death, we can see the reflection of life gazing back at us. Sometimes, as in the case of Peter Samuelson, we can become aligned with our own unique destiny. Through meeting Sean, a young boy dying from an inoperable brain tumor, Peter experienced an epiphany that would change the course of his life forever. He became Sean's friend on the last part of his earthly journey, and this gesture opened the floodgates of his heart.

Summer had arrived. The day was hot and sultry, but a welcome breeze flowed off the ocean, which appeared to sparkle and shimmer far out into the horizon. The Pacific Coast Highway meanders and winds its way along the coast, providing the most magnificent views. Passing through an arc of majestic cliffs, the rhythms, beauty, and wildness of the natural world can be experienced as the vista opens up to the sight of the waves bouncing and breaking onto a shoreline of golden sand. If one is lucky enough – it is sometimes possible to pause for a moment and reflect on the wondrous sight of playful dolphins and seals bobbing their heads above the surface of the water, before heading into the materially-driven metropolis of Los Angeles.

Peter Samuelson arrived at the restaurant in Beverley Hills, which was full of lunchtime chatter as executives sat together discussing business deals, and secretaries ordered salads and chatted with their girlfriends. Peter was well dressed, charming, and friendly. Even though he had lived in the United States for a number of years, he still retained his unmistakable English accent as he recounted his story.

* * * * *

Peter

I was born in the London suburb of Hampstead. I had a happy childhood, and was raised by great parents. My grandfather had been a silent film producer, who became bankrupt when the talkies came in. As a result, my father was brought up in great poverty, and had to leave school by the age of fourteen. It was very important to him that I should receive the education he was denied, and I felt a lot of pressure on me to succeed academically.

I enjoyed high school, and worked as hard as I could. The perseverance paid off when I was offered a full scholarship to Cambridge University, where I read English Literature. At Cambridge, I first realized that life consisted of more than medieval literature. I became socially engaged and fought for changes in various pro-social ways, certainly with at best mixed success.

I stumbled into producing films, partly because as a French translator on Steve McQueen's film *Le Mans* in my Gap Year in 1970, I was never really much good at telling the other side of a meeting what I thought my guy meant, as opposed to what he actually said. Also because my father had omitted to tell me what my grandfather had told him: "Don't be a producer; it's too difficult and totally irrational".

I moved back to London after I graduated, and managed somehow to get hired repeatedly as a production manager, the senior organizer who works for the producer of a film. A Hollywood-based commercial company offered me the position of staff line producer. I thought, "This is a great opportunity," and headed out to Los Angeles. It was a struggle at first, because the UK government would only let me bring $40 with me, but I soon fell in love with the country and sensed anything was possible.

Gradually, I began to get the breaks, and started to find success as a producer. My movies did well. I produced *Revenge of the Nerds* and *Turk 182*, and then I partnered with my brother, Marc, and made *Arlington Road*, *Wilde*, *Tom and Viv* and other films, which gave me a sense of creative accomplishment as well as an income. But I had a nagging realization that the all-encompassing and mostly self-absorbed studio mentality left a void in my life. I think that you can go nuts as a film producer. You can mislay your compass, lose your sense of direction and fall over the edge of the cliff, onto the jagged dangerous rocks of delusion and narcissism below. I see it happening all the time in this business.

I had no idea of how to fill this void, but everything changed by fluke in the fall of 1982, when I had a conversation with my cousin, the actress Emma Samms. When Emma was still living in London, she had lost her brother, my cousin Jamie, to an awful disease called Aplastic Anaemia. While visiting Great Ormond Street Children's Hospital later, she had come to know and befriend a young boy, Sean, who was fighting an inoperable brain tumor. She told me about him, saying:

> Sean is such a brave and remarkable young kid. He's gone through so much in his young life, but he lights up when he tells me about his secret longing to visit Disneyland before he dies. I really wish there was something I could do to make his wish come true. I know what a difference this trip would make to him. Unfortunately, there's no way his mother could afford for him to go.

As Emma related the story to me, I was moved. It reminded me of one of the most devastating memories of my teenage years, when Jamie had contracted his illness and ultimately died. There was enormous pain for all the family; Jamie's father searched for cures all over the world but at the time, sadly, none existed. We all had to witness a vital, intelligent and greatly loved child just waste away. I always remember the shattering sight of such a very small coffin at his funeral.

I said to Emma, "Let's make Sean's dream come true. Let's arrange to fly him and his mother over and make the dream a reality." Shortly after, Sean and his mother arrived in Los Angeles. We couldn't find a hotel that would accommodate such a sick child, so I moved them all into my condominium, including Emma.

It was wonderful to see how Sean rallied, despite how far advanced his illness was. There was a look of wonder and excitement on his face, as we visited Disneyland and all the other attractions. We even borrowed a helicopter and pilot, so that he could see Los Angeles from the air.

For a while time stood still. Sean's illness faded into the background, and I think that for the first time in a long while, he got to experience feelings of pure joy. The trip also had a domino effect. Sean's mother began to relax, and found great enjoyment in watching her son having so much fun. It was touching to see how happy this made Sean, for seeing his mother relaxed and carefree just served to increase his own high spirits.

Sean returned to London, and died a few weeks later. I experienced a very complex set of emotions after his death. I felt enormous sadness, because he lived in my condo, and I had been privileged to share such an incredible experience with him. But we had all been preparing for the inevitable, including Sean himself, and there was a good feeling knowing that we had crammed so many unforgettable moments into his last days. I also knew that his mother had been blessed with the most precious gift. She had memories of her son laughing and transcending his illness, rather than just fading away in a hospital bed.

Some time later, I was having lunch with a business acquaintance from HBO named Steve Ujlaki. We were meeting to discuss a project. Halfway through the lunch, we ran out of business to discuss, and Steve said, "So what else is going on in your life?" I replied, "Well, the strangest thing happened to me, there was this little boy..."

I told him the rest of the story and, as Steve listened, he broke down and wept at the table. For a moment, it just all seemed horrendously embarrassing — for him, for me, and for the people sitting at the next table. But suddenly, I felt this tremendous surge of energy flow through me; it was almost as if I had been struck by lightning. The experience with Sean had been so powerful for me, but now I realized that the story could also have a colossal emotional effect on someone else. I left the lunch feeling overwhelmed by the enormity of what had taken place, and for a couple of weeks just let everything stew around inside me.

One morning, I woke up and knew that I was being called to start a children's charity for kids like Sean. It was conceived initially as an organization that would grant seriously ill children their wish. Although I had no doubts about the validity of this mission, I asked myself, "How on earth am I going to do this? I've got no idea how to launch a charity." Then I thought, "Well, I have skills as a film producer, and I'm used to working against the odds, so I can use these same skills to make this project work and get it off the ground."

I recognized that I would need a lawyer, an accountant, a publicist, a fundraiser, and someone who knew all about hospital policies. I spent the rest of the day calling everyone that   might help, and arranged a meeting for that afternoon.

We all met in the Interscope boardroom; I stood there and told them about Sean and how I believed that we could make something similar happen for other seriously ill children. Everyone listened to what I had to say, and there was complete silence in the room. Then the most amazing scene took place, as they all agreed to my proposal and that was just the beginning!

Fate was definitely taking a hand in my life that day. Previously, I had gone out on a date with a lady who was accountant, and I had asked her to the gathering. When the lawyer asked, "What are we going to call this organization?" She replied, "You remember the children's rhyme that goes *Star light, star bright, first star I see tonight?* We all nodded, and she added, "How about calling the charity *Starlight?* We all agreed that this was the perfect name. You could say that the meeting was our second date, because we fell in love and have been together ever since. She became the first treasurer of the organization.

The *Starlight Children's Foundation* has grown into an international nonprofit organization dedicated to improving the quality of life for seriously ill children and their families. The charity just snowballed, and we can now serve over 2.5 million children every year, on an annual budget of around 40 million dollars. We have chapters and affiliates in Japan, Australia, Canada, the U.K., and right across the United States, and we provide an array of important psycho-social services to seriously ill children and their families. It is a colossus!

As *Starlight* began to flourish, I started to see that there was far more we could do for seriously ill children. One day, I was visiting the County-USC Medical Center in Los Angeles. As I walked through the facility, I came across a child's room, and the only source of entertainment was an old black and white television mounted on the wall.

I asked the nurse, "How's this child in traction meant to change the channel?"

"I'll show you," she replied. She went over to a corner in the room and brought out a seven-foot long bamboo pole that the child was supposed to use to watch another program.

"Surely we can do better than this?" I said to myself. And, with the help of Michael Milken, I invented *Starlight Fun Centers*, which are composed of entertainment centers set in portable carts that can be rolled onto a child's bed. Then I thought about the children lying in bed all day with nothing to do, and thought it might be possible to formulate some unique programming that would keep them amused and stimulated.

As I mused over this idea, I decided that we needed to expand our mission to develop this kind of programming. I knew that we would need a powerful ally in our corner, somebody who wouldn't be intimidated by the major studios. Kathy Kennedy, one of our first board members, managed to arrange for me to have a meeting with Steven Spielberg. When I arrived at his office, his assistant said, "Be brief, and get right to the point." She added, "Mr. Spielberg can only give you fifteen minutes of his time." I felt totally intimidated! However, my fifteen minutes turned into over two hours and Steven was totally engaged, as we kicked ideas around for what we called *Starbright*. The he said:

"I think it's an incredible project. Count me in. How can I help?"

I replied, "I think you would be the perfect person to chair *Starbright* and help recruit experts for the board. We also desperately need a financial contribution."

"How much do you want?" Steven asked.

At that moment, a voice that sounded like mine, but came from an unknown source deep within me, uttered the words, "Two and a half million dollars."

"You've got it," said Steven.

I left the meeting knowing that we had all the backing needed to succeed in this new activity, which would creatively bring so many rays of sunshine into the lives of sick children.

I get enormous rewards from my involvement in this kind of work, because I get to see the results of trying to make a difference in the lives of these children. I opened the mail this morning and received a copy of American Airlines' *Advantage* magazine. On the front cover, there was a picture of a kid in a wheelchair, with Mickey Mouse standing next to him and the caption read: "American Airlines and the Starlight Foundation sent this child to Disney World." I thought, "This is great. I had a hand in making that happen, and it's totally wonderful. What an honor, what a privilege in a nutty world."

My belief is that we can all make a contribution in trying to make the world a better place. And through choosing to become involved, we also lift ourselves up and build our own happiness. A friend approached me recently, saying:

"Peter, my boyfriend is moving to New York, and I have no friends in the city. I don't know what to do. Can you suggest anything?"

Without hesitating, I replied, "Did you know that besides helping 200,000 sick children a month, *Starlight* is one of the most remarkable dating services that I've ever heard of? We've had so many marriages that I can't remember them all. If you want to meet genuine, good people, get involved with a charity, my dear!"

Of course, it's not all plain sailing. There's the constant stress of never having enough money, volunteers, or time, and there is always so much more to be done. Through becoming involved, I have learned of some truly shocking statistics:

In America, a million children at any one time are in foster care, institutions, or on the streets. Over 1,000 children die every year through abuse or neglect, and an average of 1,690 children are sexually assaulted each week. One in six children lives in poverty. Over half the children who appear at an official hearing, where their whole life is held in the balance, have no lawyer.

I was horrified and deeply upset at this state of affairs. And then I became angry, and wondered what could be done to improve the situation. It seemed an enormous task, but like I tell my own kids, "If you're not willing to fail, you can't possibly succeed." So, I established a new organization called *First Star*, whose mission it is to improve the life outcomes of America's abused and neglected children. Through research and raising the public's awareness, our vision is to provide quality and compassionate care for children in every aspect of the system. In this, the richest nation in the world, how can we do anything else?

I still feel the stress and frustration of wanting to do more. Every day, we can look around and see someone who needs a helping hand. Most weekends, I ride my bike from the village down to the beach. It's about a fifteen-mile trip, and one Sunday I counted forty-one homeless people along the way. Most of them carted their possessions around in a stolen shopping cart, and slept in a large cardboard box. I started to think about the challenges these people face, and realized that most of them had to do with finding shelter in bad weather.

After pondering on the problem for a while, I arranged a meeting with the Pasadena Art Center College of Design, and I sponsored a competition to see if some of the students could come up with a better idea than giving men, women and children the empty cardboard box that a refrigerator came in. They submitted some great designs and our fourth prototype EDAR ("Everyone Deserves A Roof") will be in Beta testing on the streets shortly. It's similar to a shopping cart, but it has retractable panels that convert into a tent to give a bed and protection from the elements at night. Of course it's not as good as being able to offer people a permanent home, but it's a great improvement on a cardboard box.

I often get people coming up to me, saying, "The hand of God must be working through you," or, "You must be on a mission from God." I think it disappoints them when I reply, "I'm an agnostic." Don't misunderstand me, because if I die and wake up to find myself in heaven, I will be delighted, and the first to apologize! But I've reinterpreted my own religion to be a kind of passionate Humanism, a belief that all of us have an instinct to lift up our civilization, and to make the one we leave our kids better than the one we received.

Maybe the force of a higher power is working through me, and perhaps Sean was an angel delivering a message. I just don't know the answer to that. But what I do know is that Sean was a courageous, wonderful human being and I wanted to help him. From the day I met him, there was no turning back. My life was changed forever. I do believe that there is a force in the hearts of people that can bring about our highest aspirations for civilization. We all have a role to play. When the call comes – it heralds an opportunity to search deep within ourselves to find compassion, love, and charity, and to manifest these qualities out into the world. If that is God, then count me a believer.

I know my wonderful staff and volunteers all feel the same way. They each have a purpose, and are of great intrinsic value, because they create some joy and offer help to those who need it. They provide happiness to sick kids, a helping hand to abused and neglected children, and shelter for the homeless… What could possibly be more rewarding? It's an honor to be around them.

* * * * *

Peter tells a deeply moving story that is full of hope for the future. His encounter with a dying child illustrates how engaging with death, enables life to move in such mysterious ways. Sean provided Peter with the opportunity to align himself with a sense of purpose or mission for this lifetime. Through projecting his good intentions, Peter experienced extraordinary synchronicities that gave rise to chance meetings, unexpected events and the wisdom of an unseen guiding hand that was ready to aid his humanitarian efforts.

WILMA'S STORY

A dog has the soul of a philosopher
Plato

Wilma Melville was deployed to the scene of the Oklahoma City bombing, along with her search dog, Murphy. There ensued a race against time to find survivors buried in the rubble. It was a heartbreaking experience, because there were not enough certified dog-handler teams. Wilma left the disaster scene profoundly changed by her experience. She made it her mission to rescue and train abandoned dogs for search and rescue work. The next time a catastrophe occurred, they would be ready.

Home to the National Disaster Search Dog Foundation can be found in the heart of Ojai, California. The organization's office is set in an attractive Spanish-style architectural complex, and spring can be seen in full bloom in the form of many beautiful shrubs surrounding the charming courtyard.

Several black Labradors greet visitors enthusiastically, and usher them into the office. The walls are framed with pictures of rescue dogs and their handlers at work, during the Oklahoma Bombing and Ground Zero terrorist attacks.

Wilma arrives, bursting with life and energy. Clarity and compassion are reflected in her distinctively blue eyes.

* * * * *

Wilma

I grew up with my family in Newark, New Jersey. As a child, I always loved animals, and one of my most treasured possessions is a little photo of me holding a puppy in my arms. I couldn't have been more than three or four years old when it was taken.

We had dogs at home and when I got older, I began to realize how much these animals were really capable of. There's a closeness that a dog is willing to share with a human which extends far beyond the fact that they need us to feed them, or take care of their needs. Dogs have a very generous spirit, and intuitively follow your lead. Growing up, I was a bit of a tomboy, and loved to spend my allowance on a bus trip out into the country, and then go for a ride at one of the stables. Being out in nature always gave me such a sense of freedom during my younger years.

Anyway, life happened. I went to College, got married, raised four boys and spent many years teaching. When I retired, I thought, "Okay, now it's my time. What am I going to do next?"

I had always liked the idea of working with dogs. Appreciation and respect are words that one rarely hears humans use with regard to animals, but the deeper your respect goes for them — the more they will give you, and the rewards can be great.

At the time, I happened to have a German Shepherd puppy, and I got involved in *schutzhund*, a sport where the dog is taught tracking, protection and obedience. My husband, John, was a little worried about me taking up this type of activity, because he was concerned that the dog could end up by hurting somebody, so I stopped. But I thought, "Wow this is a terrific dog, what else can she do?"

Somebody suggested search and rescue. As I began to research the subject, I realized that my dog would be a good candidate for the work, and this got me going off in an entirely new direction. Looking back, I see it was an important phase in my life, and that everything I had accomplished so far had helped me to reach this point.

I began to train with my dog, but I soon got disillusioned. The dog made hardly any progress, and some of the learning techniques were really hard on her. I wasn't enjoying being involved, and I started searching for someone who might know more. Eventually, I came across a trainer called Pluis Davern, at Sundowners Kennels, and I knew I had found an outstanding trainer. It was an awful lot of hard work, and certainly wasn't easy; the learning curve was tremendous. But the best thing was that the dogs loved the experience.

After completing the training, I started to work with *Disaster Search* and with the fire department, who were called out to urban disasters. As I became more involved, I found the work to be really rewarding. This was still just a hobby to me, but I got a second dog, and we made such good progress with the training techniques that we managed to get the FEMA certification for search and rescue dogs reduced from three years to eighteen months. I was delighted, and thought, "Well, I've reached my goal, and I've achieved everything I set out to do." But then the Oklahoma Bombing took place, and for me, it was a life-changing experience.

All of us from the world of *Search and Rescue* were watching the TV coverage, following the bombing of the Murrah Federal Building in Oklahoma City. Reports stated that two task forces with dogs had been sent in to help with the rescue operation. I said to my husband, "Two task forces will never be enough. I'm going to pack." At that moment, my pager went off and I was assigned to the Los Angeles County task force, together with my dog, Murphy.

It is almost impossible to describe the scene of a disaster like that. We are shaken out of our complacency by sudden violent death: the tragic loss of life, the anguish and the sheer scale of human suffering — no one can go through that and be the same person. Murphy did a wonderful job; she managed to locate the body of one of the victims. But it was a heart-breaking experience. There were not enough dog-handler teams. And I realized that the handlers were all civilian volunteers, whereas the firefighters had an organized chain of command.

I returned home, determined to do something to improve future search and rescue efforts. A short time later, I was giving an interview to a local author, and during the conversation; she put forward the suggestion: "Why don't you start a foundation?" She then gave me a lot of information on how this could be accomplished — and that was the beginning of the National Disaster Search Dog Foundation.

I knew that I'd have to put time and effort into the project, but had no idea of how much of my life it would take up. I thought, "Well, if I can teach someone to play soccer, I must be able to teach dogs and handlers search and rescue." I started to write down everything I knew and could teach, and put together a curriculum. I didn't foresee how the Foundation would grow, but I knew that the dogs could provide a unique and valuable service.

In California, we had about eight certified dogs, but hundreds more were needed. Of course, I hoped that nothing like Oklahoma City would ever happen again, but the dogs were also needed for search and rescue following tornadoes, mudslides, hurricanes and earthquakes.

Dogs can find people, and show you where to dig at a disaster scene. As long as the dog is still searching, people have hope and they hold on to that hope while the rescue operation continues. If there is anyone left alive, the dog will have a really high chance of finding them, and if you find just one person, it's worth it. The dogs can also locate bodies, and this is so important to families, who are desperate for news of their loved ones. Even if there are no survivors, the relatives are assured that every possible rescue effort was made.

I realized that it was the firefighters who had the discipline needed to work with the dogs and, as the Foundation got established, they began to apply through their individual departments to take the training.

There is a tremendous amount more to this work than meets the eye. At the beginning of the course, I always tell the applicants:

This training involves a change of lifestyle. If you have hobbies, when you choose to enter the program – the hobbies will be gone. You have to make a choice to really commit. This will be a transformation that goes far deeper than just working with a dog. Conscious choice is involved and once that choice has been made, you and your dog partner will bond together and this relationship will transcend almost everything in your life.

These people are macho firefighters; they are already fine people, better than most, because they have chosen a career that is service-orientated, and they are great to work with. However, I cannot tell them when they begin this work that something in their personality will have a flaw, and that this kind of program will bring it to the surface. I don't have to look for it, but I know that the individuals who become outstanding trainers are the ones who have been willing to recognize and work with this flaw.

The handler changes when he begins to work with the dog; it's a growth period, in which he has to shelve his intellect and sharpen his intuition so that he can understand what the dog is trying to tell him. When a handler finally lets go of his ego and accepts that the dog knows what it's doing; he starts to count on the dog, and respect grows. The better the trainer is, the more the dog is willing to give — and then we have a fine team.

These handlers may well spend more time with their dogs than with anyone else. This often results in improved personal relationships, because they learn to acknowledge people for having done a good job, and start to ignore the small stuff that really doesn't matter. This is the format that the handlers follow when they begin to work with a dog. Subsequently, I see them use the same philosophy with their families and friends.

I know that when a handler starts working with a dog, all his other relationships will change. So, the value is far beyond his relationship with that one dog. There is a ripple effect that is beautiful to see. Sometimes, a firefighter will ask, "Are you trying to get us into therapy?" I reply, "No, I'm just getting you to be able to work with the dog, so that you can save lives." These teams train and train, week in and week out. They are always ready to be deployed to a disaster site, where they carry on searching until called off. In recent years, female applicants have joined the firefighting teams, and have also applied for and completed training to become part of the dog-handler teams.

At the heart of the Foundation is a paradox. The very traits that make dogs unsuitable as family pets often make them ideal for disaster search. Each of our dogs has its own tale to tell. They are often on the brink of destruction, and then are rescued and transformed into rescuers themselves.

One such dog, Mace, had been tied to a railroad track, sprayed with mace and then abandoned. He was found and taken to a shelter, which unfortunately didn't have the resources or the time to rehabilitate him. Destroying him could have been the only choice, but luckily, our Foundation was able to offer another alternative, as a FEMA certified handler heard of his plight and hurried to collect him.

Mace was a male yellow Labrador, and the handler knew he had disaster search potential. He was brought to Ojai and housed with a foster family, as we designed a training program for him. To begin with it was tough going. Mace was wild, and he had been very badly abused. But after three months, he was sent to Sundowners Kennel for further training. There, with his true identity now apparent, his name was changed to Ace and he graduated with his class.

It was hard for the family who had taken care of Ace and grown to love him, because they had to hand him over to his firefighter handler. But amid the tears and laughter was the knowledge that Ace had work to do and a mission of his own to fulfill, and that they had helped to offer him a new life.

When the news came in of the monstrous attacks in New York on September 11, 2001, we were ready to go into action to help in the rescue mission. We sent thirteen canine search teams comprised of dogs and handlers. Later, the firefighters related their experiences, and one of NDSDF team members told his own personal story:

I felt excited and apprehensive at the same time. My dog, Manny, and I were getting the opportunity to use of all our training and knowledge to help those at the World Trade Center, but at the same time, I was apprehensive about leaving my family. Manny and I are normally attached to the L.A. City Task Force. But we were in Washington at the time, and were flown out on the second deployment in an Air Force transport.

When we arrived in New York, it was overwhelming. The sheer immensity of the devastation was eerie. We were surrounded by smoke, steam and twisted metal. It all felt surreal; I looked at the walls still left standing, and watched the smoke floating up. It reminded me of being in a huge cathedral.

Manny is a service dog and couldn't wait to start searching. It provided him with an opportunity to play and get rewarded, but the work was still dangerous, and that's why we train so hard. Manny is always with me, and our bags are always packed. We are ready to leave at a moment's notice. All the Foundation dogs were amazing in New York. It was incredible to experience all the support we had from the public, and all the concern for the dogs.

Although it was difficult and exhausting work, Manny watched out for me, and I watched out for him. We had vets on site who were incredibly caring and compassionate and ready to help the K9 teams, but remember, these dogs are not wusses; they train on rubble twice a week, and they're tough!

I was so proud of Manny. He worked so hard and searched through all that mangled steel. I couldn't believe it. But all the handlers felt the same; the dogs definitely rose to the occasion. Each one is trained to ignore all but human scent, and to alert his handler, when a survivor is located.

Our daily routine at Ground Zero was tough. We would have a briefing at the beginning of a shift, put on our gear and get the bus for the trip to the base of operations. We would then be on-site for the next twelve hours. At the end of the shift, the dogs would be so exhausted that they would fall asleep in our laps. Because of all the dust and hazardous materials, they would get decontaminated once we returned to the base. We would feed them, check them over, and put them to bed. We only got about four hours sleep, before setting off again.

Public support was tremendous. I couldn't believe all the supplies that people donated. We got everything from dog booties and dog food, to laundry service and work boots. It was wonderful to see the nation uniting and coming together to support and help each other in our time of need.

Personally, the experience changed me a lot. Life and my family became so much more precious, and I realized how important the K9's were. Unfortunately, we didn't save any lives this time, but disasters aren't going to stop happening. When the next one hits, be it an earthquake or terrorist attack, the chance of finding people alive is so much greater when a disaster search dog team is there. That team could be me and Manny, and I find a lot of comfort in that thought.

All of the rescue crews did an amazing job in New York. They knew there wouldn't be anyone left alive on the surface rubble, so they went down way deeper — five or six stories down, because they thought they might have a chance of finding someone down there.

I think life changed for everyone following 9/11. On the one hand, we got to witness the face of sheer evil, and on the other hand, we saw people open their hearts and unite in support and compassion, offering to help in any way they could. The valiant firefighters and other rescue crews were selfless, and many of them gave their own lives in the hope of saving others.

Shortly after the terrorist attack, I received a call from a man called Stephen Doyle. He was a member of a New York hockey team composed of firefighters. I remembered them, because they had previously sent us a donation. Stephen said, "Wilma, I have some very sad news. My best friend and team member, Timmy McSweeney, died in the line of duty at the World Trade Center, and we all want to do something to honor his memory. We'd like to sponsor a search and rescue dog, and we'd like the dog to be called *Recon*, after Timmy's fire station."

I promised that this would be done. Of course, the challenge would be to find the right dog-handler team — one that we were certain would attain certification. Beyond this, we wanted a team with charisma. In the class of 2002, we found the ideal match in firefighter, Jim Boggeri, who was paired with a yellow lab we named *Recon*. They completed their training, and were able to head out to New York, where they met with Timmy's team members, widow and children.

I received such tremendous support from all around the world, following the terrorist attacks. Rescue groups, shelters, and private breeders were all looking out for suitable search and rescue candidates. Shortly after the tragedy, a female chocolate Labrador was found abandoned in a wooded area with a litter of pups. The pups would all be adopted, but we rescued the mother, and she is now making a wonderful new life for herself. We named her Giuli, after former Mayor, Rudy Giuliani. She made a trip to New York with her handler, and visited the schools in New Jersey. The kids loved it and learned a lot. Many of the schools started to raise money to sponsor their own search and rescue dogs.

Donations came pouring in from all over the globe, and we were able to send a further twelve dogs into training, rather than just the two we had planned on. Calls come in every day, offering us potential disaster dogs. To help transport them to Ojai, we have help from American Airlines flight attendants, who support us by donating their free mileage, and flying the dog in the cabin right to us. These people are heroes in our eyes, because with this kind of cross-country connection, we can rescue a potential candidate from anywhere in the United States. Prior to the generosity of these people, many fine dogs slipped through our hands.

Most recently, following the terrible devastation caused by Hurricane Katrina, thirty-one NDSDF canine disaster search teams were deployed to the New Orleans area to help with the rescue efforts. Despite the extreme humidity, which was almost unbearable, the dogs were able to search for survivors in those areas where humans may have been able to survive. Once again, these teams did a magnificent job, and even though the conditions made it extremely tough, and dehydration was a real concern, the dogs never gave up and carried on searching through the piles of rubble throughout their twelve-hour shifts.

For many of these survivors, the presence of the dog-handler teams brought hope, and the reassurance that everything possible was being done to locate missing people. Many individuals were afraid of leaving their homes and being parted from their pets, but the teams were also able to reassure them, and help them to safety.

My only regret is that I didn't start the Foundation earlier, but it was a challenge to find out what worked. I know what we are doing has value, and I realize that all the former experiences I had in life led me to this work. If you think of something that can make a difference, my advice is: do it, and make it happen! I know that my vocation brings me great joy, and I see that this is true for all the volunteers who work alongside of me.

I think our purpose here on earth is to leave the world a slightly better place than we found it. I'm certainly no genius, but I know that when one makes a full and complete commitment, extraordinary things can happen. Boldness is part of my nature, and when I want to achieve something, I try and connect with the part of me that is bold and powerful. My husband, John, was one of my greatest supporters and upon his retirement, he worked with me for many years. It was wonderful to share such a great experience together.

Recently, we held a workshop in San Diego, and twenty-five teams of dogs and handlers carried out a drill. There were two people hidden in a fire tower, which is a practice place where firefighters set fires, one by one. A dog entered the tower to do the searching, while his handler remained outside. Once the dog had located the missing people; it alerted the handler. I looked at this group — you don't usually get the chance to see them gathered together — and I thought, "These people all look so fine, and the dogs look so good, I am so proud to have been a part of this."

* * * * *

Wilma's compassionate response following her experiences during the grueling aftermath of the Oklahoma bombing changed the course of her life forever. Her subsequent efforts to provide more rescue dogs demonstrates how respect for the animal kingdom can result in a symbiotic exchange. Once rescued from often appalling and inhumane conditions, the NDSDF dogs will never need to be rescued again. In turn, they bond with their human handlers and are trained to use their highly tuned sense of smell and their ability to navigate dangerous terrains to search for disaster victims in places that humans cannot access. These extraordinary animals love their work. They help rescue people that are trapped in the chaos and darkness of a disaster site, and bring them back to the light.

SALLY'S STORY

If a man neglects education, he walks lame to the end of his life
Plato

Sally and Donald Goodrich lost their son, Peter, on 9/11/2001. He was on board United Airlines, Flight 175, which was the second of the two planes to hit the World Trade Center. Two pilots, seven flight attendants, and fifty-six passengers also lost their lives.

Shortly before his death, Peter was reading the Qur'an to further his wide-embracing search for the meaning of life. To honor his memory as an advocate for world peace, Sally became involved in the reconstruction of a school in war-ravaged Afghanistan.

There were many different reactions across America and the rest of the world following 9/11, but the most heartening of them was when millions of people headed for libraries and bookstores and swept the shelves clean of any book that could connect them with Islam. Their intention was to reflect on Islam and Muslim societies, with the hope of gaining insight into the "bigger picture" that lay at the heart of such a tragedy. Many people came to recognize that there were many philosophical, religious and psychological issues that needed to be addressed, and that human suffering is experienced by all those who are endangered by war and violence.

* * * * *

Sally

The weekend leading into 9/11, we moved from our family home to Bennington to take care of my father, who was in the last stages of Alzheimer's disease. It was the last time we were together as a family, and encountered a temporary illusion of happiness and security. It is impossible to describe the heartbreaking tragedy of losing a child. Peter was adored by his family. He loved life and was a brilliant athlete. After graduating from High School, he attended Bates College, where he met the love of his life, Rachel, and they got married in 1992.

Peter inherited his father's size and strength but, from the time he was a small child, he displayed a kindness and tenderness that stayed with him forever. He was the kind of person who always tried to help people, and gave money to the homeless. One day, he stopped to pull some change out of his pocket and ended up in conversation with a man who didn't have any shoes, so he went back to his car and gave him a brand new pair of trainers. This charitable act sums up his character, and it's something I've never forgotten.

Peter loved being out in nature, and had a wonderful imagination. He is remembered for his enthusiasm and joy of life. He worked with intellectual Russian, Jewish, Serbian and Indian immigrants who were struggling to succeed in this culture, and embraced the insights and gifts they provided. It was no surprise to learn that he had been reading the *Qur'an* shortly before he died, for the text is said to be the sacred word of God channeled through the archangel Gabriel, and given to the Prophet Muhammad. His copy was full of markers, where passages crossed the threshold of his wondering. Peter had embarked on a wide-ranging search for answers to the meaning of life, and he had a deep respect for questions. He had researched all of the major religions, and his investigations led him to study the beliefs of the Muslim faith. It seemed to be a fitting tribute to take the first reading at his memorial service from the *Qur'an*.

We gathered at the service to celebrate Peter's short life. Of course, we would rather have had him still with us, but the events of 9/11 permanently changed our lives and those of families and communities all across America. We willed ourselves through the days and nights that followed; the deconstruction of our lives went on for months, as faith, trust, and hope fell victim to the ravages of grief.

Eventually, we felt the need to become involved, and do something positive. My husband, Donald, became President of Families of 9/11, and was able to use his three decades of experience as a lawyer, in order to help lobby for greater compensation for the families of victims, and to attempt to find out what really happened.

We set up the Peter M. Goodrich Foundation with the intention of doing something that would make a difference. In August of 2004, Major Rush Filson, a childhood friend of Peter's, went on a voluntary tour of duty in Afghanistan. While there, he saw a desperate need within the school system. In a letter home, he outlined the plight of the Afghan schoolchildren, and told of an Afghan teacher he had met, saying:

The man runs a school that has three hundred students, in a little mud compound next to a house that is owned by one of the wealthiest men in the village. The benefactor doesn't charge any rent, but that's the limit of his generosity, for there isn't any water and no sanitary facilities are available. This teacher has become a target, because he's the leader of an institution of conventional learning. Cloaked men have burst into his house at night, threatening the lives of his entire family. He responds every time by telling them that they can kill him, but until they do, he'll continue to teach. He also has the difficult task of telling his staff every month that he cannot pay them, because he can't get funds.

Hearing this courageous story was a moment of grace; a door opening. Peter's essence was my compass, and for the first time, I could feel his assuring spirit. At the end of his letter, Rush said, "Try to encourage people to send school supplies." Donald and I discussed this request for aid, and thought, "Let's donate some items through the Foundation."

The schools were based in tents, and although they had plastic containers to preserve the materials from the snow, they had nowhere to store them. A friend, Kathleen Rafiq, who was at the time a TV producer in Santa Barbara, California, said, "Why not build a school in Afghanistan?" Following this conversation, I thought, "Well this is a giant leap of faith, but let's go for it." Things just snowballed and took off from there.

The school we chose to rebuild came from a recommendation from the 9/11 commission, who had put forward the idea that the United States should become involved in the reconstruction of Afghanistan. The basic structure already existed, but consisted of three rooms — each no bigger than a bedroom — set in the courtyard of an old home. Most of the building was uninhabitable, and the girls who attended the school had to drink water from a stream, as someone had stolen their pump. In Muslim societies, girls are not given the same opportunities as boys, so we decided on a school for girls.

With help from David Edwards, who was a close friend of the Afghan Deputy Interior Minister, we gained permission to secure land to build on, and the community elders approved the plans for the proposed new building.

We needed to fund the project, and the public response was amazing. Schools, churches, and community groups started to raise money. During the following months, we received over $200,000 in donations that would be used to modernize the school. The building would house sixteen class-rooms, and cater for children from kindergarten through eighth grade.

The adventure began in April, 2005. I left the security of my privi-leged life in the United States to visit Afghanistan, with my friend Kathleen Rafiq. We were excited, and looking forward to seeing how the project was progressing. In Kabul, we were met by a variety of civilian security forces and introduced to Shahmahmood, the Deputy Minister of the Interior. He constantly works at a brutal pace, dealing with long lines of officials waiting with hundreds of different petitions.

Dressed in the traditional clothes of Muslim women, complete with veils, we set off to visit the Wonkai Village in Wardak, which is set in semi-arid hilly terrain about forty minutes south of Kabul. We drove through rough terrain, and the journey was rugged; it reminded me of riding a bumper car in an amusement park back home. We passed three checkpoints on the highway, and were told to remove our sunglasses and make sure our veils were in place. We were also advised to keep our eyes down. We then passed through a string of villages leading to a valley that was surrounded by snow-covered mountain peaks. It was peaceful and beautiful, reminiscent of an ancient Biblical scene.

Having arrived at our destination, we visited a single-floor school composed of eight classrooms. It had been built by a nonprofit organization based in the United States. We were guided through the classrooms, and at the recess, I got to shake hands with the children, who were excited and trying to get my attention. I felt nostalgic, and thought, "It doesn't matter where you are in the world, because the sounds and sights of children coming to school are the same everywhere."

The village has a single Russian combine engine to generate electricity. It lights the village for four hours each evening. There is one tractor that serves as a snow plough and is also used to till the earth. Water is in short supply; one tank is used constantly, to water plants and crops, and supply the villagers with water. Gas is expensive, and every resource is precious and irreplaceable.

One of the highlights of this visit was to meet a Kuchi tribe of nomads, who were camped in tents below the village. Although we were accompanied by two soldiers with rifles; we were received with only kindness from these extraordinarily shy people, who allowed us to take pictures of them and their animals.

We were given a guided tour of most of the homes in the village, by a handsome former Mujahedin Commander, named Saraj. For the first time since Peter's death, an understanding of the great mystery of life returned, as Saraj stopped briefly and prayed with one of the children. It was a sense of spirituality which was reflective of Peter's broader view of the human experience — an inclusive view of God/Allah and the universe.

This community was struggling, and badly needed to develop small business ventures to supply a steady stream of income; they hope to obtain six sewing machines and a small building, so that widows from the war can sew clothing and becomes self-supporting.

In the evening, we were entertained by extended family members in a local home, where the women served tea and cookies. In an open courtyard, the men began dancing with more grace than I could ever have managed, or imagined. We were treated like royalty, and I thought, "It will be so difficult to leave here and return home. I'm definitely a village girl at heart."

Throughout the day, we had heard the calls to prayer that were sung by a voice which traveled up the valley, serving as a constant reminder of our place in the world. I went to bed that night surrounded by the images and thoughts of everything that I had experienced.

I woke up at dawn, and ventured off alone to investigate the surrounding area, only to lose my balance and trip on some stones. I fell hard on my face; blood was dripping down the side of my head, and dirt and mud caked my clothes and hair. Saraj was upset; he gave me a lecture, saying: "This is very, very bad. All you do is fall. You cannot come back here, for you may end up breaking an arm or a leg." I begged and pleaded with him, and said, "Please let me come back — next time I'll bring my husband with me." But he would not listen to any of my explanations or apologies.

Eventually, after a bucket bath, I thought I'd go out and try to placate Saraj, who sternly said, "Put a scarf over your head when you are outside." It took him quite a while to calm down, and we packed up reluctantly. Saraj lined up the orphans; they presented me with a wall hanging and shook my hand. Afghanistan is a dangerous place for an American woman, and I knew that Saraj had been worried for my safety.

We drove through the checkpoints and were back into the rush of human life and activity that makes up Kabul. There were little stalls everywhere that sold everything from construction materials to food and car parts. Dust covered everything, and a thick layer of smog filled the sky. Kabul appeared like a colony of red ants after the rains — full of refugees and reconstruction. Life was all about survival.

The next morning, I was seventh in line for the bucket bath before heading off to Logar, to visit the area where our school was located. We drove with Shahmahmood, and it felt like riding around with the President, as we were escorted by a caravan of security cars. We headed south of Wardak into a broad, lush and fertile valley, with steep mountains rising up on either side. Saraj, who accompanied us, said, "When the Russians invaded Afghanistan, the province of Logar suffered horrific casualties, because there was no place to hide." I nodded and replied, "Well, that gives us even more of a reason to build there."

We stopped at a gas station, and an elder greeted us. He told us that when Taliban or Mujahedin fighters had stopped to fill up with gas, his son had been murdered for asking the soldiers for payment. I felt a great sympathy for this man's story and the terrible loss he had suffered, as thoughts of Peter filled my mind.

The road to the school was paved; it was situated just off the highway, and a beautiful brook ran by the site. It was a large plot, and I silently prayed my, "Don't fall, go slow, watch your feet" mantra. We arrived to find that the school foundation was complete, and designed to withstand earthquakes as well as accommodate a third story when the time came. I was delighted by the decisions that had been made, and the planning that had taken place.

We moved on to the current girls' school, and were invited up some well-worn steps to the Principal's office. She and I exchanged smiles, and then we visited a row of classrooms that were crowded with children. In one room, two grades of children sat side by side, in nearly impossible teaching conditions. It was clear that one of the teachers was asking Shahmahmood, "Who is this woman?" He explained, and the subject of 9/11 came up in their conversation. I could see that she was visibly moved as she looked over in my direction.

Two groups of girls were asked to sing, and their young voices sounded so beautiful. Then we listened as one of them was asked to read. It was an incredible visit, and just before leaving, we were handed gifts: a beaded pencil from a shy art teacher, and a red heart-shaped box that contained rhinestone earrings, necklace, and ring. I decided to save the jewelry to wear on the anniversary of 9/11.

We then went back down the stairs to an open courtyard. Portions of the house were not safe for occupancy, so three large classes of first, second, and third grade students were working side by side under tents. Even in early spring, they were already too warm, and I was heartened as I thought, "We are building a school for children who badly need a facility."

Shahmahmood estimated that more money was needed in order to purchase furniture to fit out the new school. His goal was to build a model school with a walkway and playground, so I knew there would be more fundraising to do when we returned home.

We stopped again in Kabul, to look around the many stalls and buy some souvenirs. But the financial need of all Afghanistan is so great that I could not justify spending money on trinkets, and I thought, "The children at Sullivan Elementary will understand when I explain to them why I'm not returning home laden with Afghan artifacts."

In four short days, my worldview had been changed. All I could think of was that the people of Wardak had to buy a tire for their tractor that would cost $1,000. In order to save money, someone had to drive all the way to Herat, a considerable distance, just to try to get a good deal.

I had deep respect for Shahmahmood and all the people I was privileged to meet in Wardak, Logar and Kabul. They displayed great optimism for their future, despite past suffering and inadequate resources.

A couple of days later, we were driven to the province of Kapisa, where we would visit the site for a new school designed exactly like ours. Hopefully, in the future there will be many similar schools built all over the country. We set off towards the snow-capped Hindu Kush mountain range. Eventually, we left the paved road for an undulating dirt road surrounded by hillocks that reminded me of the slopes of a nearby ski area back home. At the base of the mountains, deep broad gullies carved by spring runoffs were evident along both sides of the road. I wondered to myself, "How on earth do they manage to build roads under such circumstances?"

We then crossed a bridge that led into a beautiful village with open shops that were so close to the car that you could reach out and touch them. The residents were delighted to see us, as we slowly snaked up the winding road that led to open pastures, farms, and animals. We dead-ended in a small collection of buildings situated on the slope of a hill that overlooked a nearby mountain range. The scenery was breathtaking; it was verdant, secluded, and pastoral —appearing even more beautiful than the village in Wardak, which had previously stolen my heart.

A large crowd had assembled, and a small girl's choir greeted us. Flowers were thrown over our heads and, at that moment, Shahmahmood reminded me of Gandi because he is also a thoughtful, spiritual man who is working for the peaceful restoration of his country. I was given a comfortable chair, and a passage from the *Qur'an* was intoned by a soloist, before Shahmahmood led a massive crowd to view an open foundation for the new building.

I was called forward to cross a shaky metal bridge that was about six feet wide and spanned the foundation. I was given a small stone to be cemented alongside others that had been placed there After all the celebrations, we left the area and returned to Wardak, which now almost felt like home.

Suddenly, the day of departure loomed before me and I was awakened by Mufti, the guard dog patrolling the area. At breakfast, I tried to recite a Frost poem from a book that I was leaving as a gift for Saraj, but Kathleen started to cry before I could reach the end.

I stood gazing over the village thinking of all the wonderful people I had met, and places that I'd seen. I knew Afghanistan was the right place for love and for the expression of the love that Peter gave so generously to everyone who had the privilege of having known him. No place on earth could have served his memory better.

As the plane thundered along the runway, I left my heart and thoughts in this country of great hospitality, humor and grace that was so readily expressed, even in the face of extreme hardship and suffering. Hope and development were rampant in all the provinces I'd seen. This visit had been the experience of a lifetime, which gave new meaning to all that we take for granted in the United States. Even though I felt emotional to be leaving, I also felt uplifted, because I knew that we were participating in the rebuilding of an amazingly beautiful country and an exquisite culture.

Prior to the beginning of our project, I could not read anything about Afghanistan or Islam. Now, I found myself comforted by little else. I wanted to learn everything about the culture, traditions, religion and codes of honor of these remarkably resilient people.

I returned to Afghanistan six months later to see how the school was progressing; it was the perfect place to spend the fourth anniversary of September 11. There was an air of festivity all around Kabul, as the country was getting ready for its first parliamentary election. Posters were everywhere: across the streets on wires, high up in trees and all over vehicles.

Logar's broad plain was greener than I remembered. The mountains still climbed from the valley floor to the heavens. Tasseled cornfields and apple orchards lined the road, and reminded me of home. As we turned into the existing school, the girls were leaving and waving. I gave the principal an album that contained Kathleen's pictures from the previous visit, and included photographs of all the churches and schools back home that were involved in contributing to the effort.

Then we moved on to the new school. I stood there amazed, thinking, "It's huge. There's no other word." The school will have twenty-five rooms and house sixteen classrooms, plus a wonderful entryway which will serve as a deck on the second floor, for the Principal to address the students. The views from the windows were made for daydreamers like

Peter, and will compete for any student's attention. The brick is now covered with concrete, but in the remaining section yet to be covered, a slight gap between the walls was evident, which would provide for movement during earthquakes.

The rooms were blessedly cool, and the schoolyard rivals most back home; it is surrounded by a high stone security wall that required as much construction material as the school itself. Near a dry riverbed, the foundation extends well below the waterline. By the end of the tour, I understood the enormous scope of the project. Midway through our visit, Shahmahmood said, "The school is going to be dedicated to Peter." I was completely taken aback and needed a small detour, to integrate my overwhelming emotional response.

We ended the day sitting in my favorite apple orchard, listening for a time to the echoes of a nearby Imam teaching the *Qur'an* to village boys. Once lessons were over, the Imam and his students joined us. Across from me, I saw the brother of the foreman; I had met him on my last visit, and felt uniquely connected to him, because his son had also been murdered. He asked me how old Peter was, when he died. I returned the question, and he told me that his son had been twenty-two when he was killed. Behind him were his two young and beautifully behaved grandchildren, who were quietly playing. They were the children of his deceased son.

We were sampling apples from the orchard and roasting corn. I was hesitant to finish mine, because I had been suffering from an upset stomach earlier in the day. As I returned the cob, partially eaten, to my plate, my soul mate (for lack of a better word) picked up my unfinished food and began to eat the remaining pieces. Shahmahmood translated the meaning of this action, saying, "It is a sign of respect to eat the remnants of food from an honored guest." This was one of the many touching moments of such an incredible day, and helped me to value Islam as it is practiced in the villages of the countryside.

Following Peter's death, my experiences in Afghanistan helped me to transition from grief back into life. I was the recipient of love, and it felt like walking through a door; on one side was grief, on the other a greater understanding of life as a result of suffering, which is the universal language that prepares us for greater insight. It felt like a choice that was guided by being in touch with Peter's spirit or essence, for he was all about love. With trepidation, we had relentlessly pursued the truth while never losing sight of Peter's respect for life, in all its manifestations. It was really his journey, one taken in his stead. He would have done the same for us, if we had been on that plane. I have seen the rugged beauty of a country and culture that has never been truly valued and met noble generous people, who have helped me to understand the circumstances that laid the foundations of 9/11. I remain committed to continuing the much-needed work to restore a country, but the needs are beyond the imagination.

I now have an Afghan child living in my home, who reminds us of how our family used to be. At a recent Service Learning High School Concert, I reflected on my experience, saying:

Thank you for helping me recall Peter's gentle and intellectually curious spirit which, for me, is evident in the work on display. Let me end by borrowing from the book *Hannah Coulter*, by Wendell Berry. Even dead, Peter is the man I remember, not as he was, but as he is: alive in my love. Death is a sort of lens, although until this fall, I used to think of it as a wall or a shut door. Death changes things and makes them clearer, and maybe it is the truest way of knowing this dream, this brief and timeless life. At times, when my life slowly fills with silence, Pete's absence comes into it and fills it. I suffer my hard joy. I give my thanks. I cry my cry. And then, I turn again to that other world that you have taught me to know, the world that is neither past, nor to come — the present world, where we are alive together and love keeps us.

* * * * *

The fifth anniversary of 9/11 arrived in 2006. For Sally, her family and all of those who lost a loved one in the terrorist attacks which took place in New York, The Pentagon, and Pennsylvania, it was a day of mourning, as they reflected and remembered a day that changed the fabric of their lives forever. In New York, dawn broke solemnly over the barren sixteen-acre site which is all that remains following the devastation caused by the jetliners that crashed into the twin towers, claiming so many lives. Family and friends gathered with photos and flowers. They were joined by firefighters and members of other rescue organizations, pausing to remember fallen comrades who selflessly gave their lives in the valiant rescue attempts. Four minutes of silence were observed to mark the times at which the jetliners plunged into the buildings, and the exact moment when each tower fell. In churches and vigils throughout the world, people also paused in respect and sympathy.

To overcome and transcend grief, pain and anger, and manifest the courage to help those in war-ravaged Afghanistan was an enormous act of faith. But for Sally, it opened the doorway to healing and the emergence of her higher self. Peter made his presence felt, and will remain alive in the hearts of all of the children who, through his death, were ultimately touched by his life.

BIRTH, DEATH, AND REBIRTH:

A CONTINUUM OF CONSCIOUSNESS

You too, gentlemen of the jury, must look forward to death
with confidence
Plato

In considering the concept of a continuum of consciousness that includes an afterlife, it is important to look to ancient civilizations, who had no problem understanding their place in the cosmos. They lived in close harmony with the rhythms of the natural world, in which all forms of animal and plant life were, as they believed, connected. Through observing natural cycles, these people were able to make sense of the mysteries of birth, death, and rebirth. They understood the symbolic analogy that nature provided, which enabled them to experience and feel a cosmic, numinous, sacred higher power that guided the workings of the universe. Life was considered to be a continuum of consciousness, controlled by a form of psychic energy that manifested in symbolic metaphors. It was during this period that archetypal divinities made their presence felt in human consciousness.

The natural world provided and instilled a feeling of "oneness" with an expanded form of consciousness, because nature constantly has the ability to renew itself, and with every death, there follows resurrection. This constant cycle of regeneration symbolized the eternal life of the soul, and there were many examples. Each evening, the dying sun — often at its most luminous point — descended and set like a golden globe on the horizon. This is the place where the sky meets the earth, and a fine white line symbolizes the sheerest of veils, that separates the visible from the invisible worlds. Every morning, the sun was reawakened; born again at dawn. The moon was also constantly reborn, and renewed itself each month. The shore of the ocean was hidden and then exposed by the turn of the unceasing incoming and outgoing tides, and the barren starkness of winter gave way to the reemergence of spring and new life.

The analogy of the *Tree of Life* also provided an image of both the macrocosm and the microcosm, instilling a "magical" sense of connection to the primordial origins and divine roots of human existence. In *Man's Search for Meaning*, Viktor Frankl illustrates how this sacred connection can still be accessed: He relates the experience of a young woman who was dying in the Nazi camps. Through the window of her hut, she could see a single branch of a chestnut tree that had two blossoms in flower. The tree offered her comfort and great solace, and she remarked to Frankl:

This tree here is the only friend I have in my loneliness. I often talk to this tree…It said to me, 'I am here – I am here – I am life, eternal life'.

Nature's capacity for renewal was illustrated through myth, for the ancient Gods died during the summer solstice, as the sun descended into the depths of winter and crossed the threshold into the underworld. At the winter solstice, the Gods were seen to reappear in the sky, as the returning sun heralded the promise and stirrings of new life. As Tamara Andrews states in the *Dictionary of Nature Myths:*

Because the setting sun disappeared in the west, its death made the western horizon a door to the Underworld. Through the door was a place of darkness, a place where serpents and snakes fought battles to retain the dying gods and extinguish the light of the sun. They never succeeded for the dying gods and the sun were immortal.

In modern-day Western society, sacred connection to the natural world no longer exists, as the ability to maintain our relationship and sense of wonder with these symbolic images is no longer a part of human consciousness. We now try to control the forces of nature, and view ourselves as set apart, rather than as being a part of the teeming life force on the planet. As a result, the ability to connect with our Divine legacy has been lost, and people are unaware of and unable to recognize the archetypal images that manifest all around us. But it is this symbolic imagery that provides an understanding of the meaning of existence, and can promote a desire to be fully involved in the process of conscious living and dying — trusting in the promise of resurrection.

Unfortunately, the voice of the natural world and its divinities can no longer be heard, and Jung described people as only able to *refer* to a belief, because they had lost this primordial understanding. This lack of connection and knowledge has resulted in a loss of meaning in life, for as Jung stated in the book *The Earth Has a Soul*: "we have stripped all things of their mystery and numinosity; nothing is holy anymore."

Reconnecting with these ancient myths and primordial images enables us to once more recognize the soul in nature, and to reacquaint ourselves with the understanding that our own soul is merely clothed in the physical body, and emanates from the same life force that is visible everywhere in the natural world. Jung believed that the soul yearned to be reunited with the supreme Light and higher power that manifests in the universe. On his travels through Africa and Egypt, he stated, "I understand that within the soul from its primordial beginnings there has been a desire for the light...the longing for light is the longing for consciousness."

Jung went on to describe that in his childhood, reverence for and connection to the natural world still existed. People recognized that animals are highly intuitive and able to sense the subtle signs that denoted oncoming storms and other changes in the environment. He also recalled that individuals at that time retained the capability to be similarly aware, and to experience prophetic dreams which would, for example, foresee an individual's death. There were also instances when a clock would stop at the moment of death, or glasses would shatter at that very second. Jung lamented that today's people no longer experience such natural occur-rences, and have no understanding of the real world that is alive in rivers, oceans, mountains, and nature in general. As a result, human beings cannot hear the voice of God, in his many names and guises — and live their lives in exile, with only unconscious stirrings to remind them of their true purpose and ultimate destiny.

Indigenous cultures experienced the sacred portal that connects the visible and invisible worlds through shamanism. The near-death experience reflects the ecstatic journey of the shaman, whose origins date back to over 30,000 years. The word *shaman* originated from the term *saman*, used by the ancient cultures that inhabited Siberia, and was translated to mean the ability to enter an altered state of consciousness and undergo an out-of-body experience resulting in feelings of ecstasy. Like the individual who experiences an NDE, the shaman moves in and out of the different realms of reality, and is able to communicate with other spirit forms. For these people, respect and a deep affinity for the natural world was reflected through the donning of animal skins and masks in order to achieve the trance-like state and become one with the ancestors. As Mircea Eliade points out in *Shamanism: Archaic States of Ecstasy*, it is through these practices that "a man becomes something far greater and stronger than himself."

In Greek mythology, Orpheus was seen to represent the figure of the first shaman, whose beautiful music and poetry could calm even the most ferocious of beasts. There are many similarities between Orpheus and Jesus Christ, for the myth of Orpheus also conveys a fundamental Christian belief in the eternal life of the soul. Orpheus' descent into the Underworld to retrieve his dead wife, Eurydice, led to his eventual death and dismemberment. However, his severed head was still singing as it was flung into the River Hebrus; this imagery symbolized a continuation of consciousness. Plato, when referring to the myth of Er, describes how Orpheus was seen to be reborn, and chose the future life of a swan. Orpheus is seen to represent the ability of the shaman to channel energy from a divine source, and obtain direct experiential knowledge concerning an afterlife state. Although these shamanic practices have largely died out in modern, westernized countries like Japan, Korea and

Taiwan, there are still shamanic practitioners who contact the spirits of the dead with impressive results.

From an early period, the religious traditions of India also included mystical, transpersonal practices in order to bring about direct experiential knowledge of an afterlife or continuing state of consciousness. This is shown by the discovery of small sculpted figures in Yoga-type postures, found on ancient seals from the great Indus Valley civilization in northwestern India. These seals date from the second millennium B.C.E. Shamanic influences are also present in these seals, and this has led scholars to believe that an early practice of Yogic meditation was combined with a type of shamanism in ancient India.

In common with shamans, the adepts of Yoga in India and Tibet — both Hindu and Buddhist — were able to develop the power of this magical flight. The idea that saints, yogins and magicians can fly is to be found everywhere in India. As Mircea Eliade states in *Shamanism: Archaic States of Ecstasy:*

Ascension and magical flight have a leading place among the popular beliefs and mystical techniques of India. Rising into the air flying like a bird, traveling immense distances in a flash, disappearing – these are some of the magical powers that Buddhism and Hinduism attribute to arhats, kings and magicians... The conception is of course, one of "pure lands," of a mystical space that has at once the nature of a "paradise" and of an "interior space."

Among many cultures, the soul is conceived of as a bird. Eliade describes how magical flight assumes the value of an "escape from the body;" and translates the ecstasy, of the liberation of the soul. But while the majority of human beings are changed into birds only at the moment of death — when they forsake their bodies and fly into the air — shamans, sorcerers, and ecstatics of all kinds realize "emergence from the body" in this world as often as they wish. The myth of the bird-soul contains the whole metaphysics of man's spiritual autonomy and freedom. While contemplating his own death, which was always imminent in the concentration camp, Viktor Frankl recalls how he managed to transcend the hopelessness of his desperate situation through psychically communicating with his beloved wife, whose essence seemed to appear before him in the form of a bird. He said:

> I had the feeling that I was able to touch her, able to stretch out my hand and grasp her. The feeling was very strong; she was *there*. Then at that very moment, a bird flew down silently and perched just in front of me, on the heap of soil which I had dug up from the ditch, and looked steadily at me.

According to Siberian practices of shamanism, it is the Dyak shaman who takes on the form of a bird in order to accompany the souls of the deceased into the afterlife.

In the Tibetan Buddhist tradition, there is an "emergence from the body" technique known as Pho-wa. Dr. Evans-Wentz describes this ability in his book *Tibetan Yoga*:

> Mastery of the Art of *Pho-wa* primarily confers the yogic power to bring about in oneself, at will, essentially the same process as that which under normal conditions is called death, there being the difference that in natural death this principle of consciousness departs from the human form permanently, whereas in yogically induced death the departure may be but temporary.

The sacred texts of *The Tibetan Book of the Dead* that were discovered buried in the Gampo hills of Central Tibet, reiterate the concept that life and death are constant states of renewal, and the Pho-wa technique is part of a transitional guidance process through which the deceased is liberated to another form of consciousness via hearing the recitation of the bardo.

Chogyam Trungpa, Rinpoche reminds us that:

> What happens when we die seems like the study of a myth; we need some practical experience of this continual process of bardo. There is the conflict between body and consciousness, and there is the continual experience of death and rebirth. There is also the experience of the bardo of dharmata, the luminosity, and of the bardo of becoming, of future possible parents, or grounding situations. We also have the visions of the wrathful and peaceful divinities, which are happening constantly, at this very moment. If we are open and realistic enough to look at it in this way, then the actual experience of death and the bardo state will not be either purely a myth or an extraordinary shock, because we have already worked with it and become familiar with the whole thing.

Belief in an afterlife is found in most religions around the world, and an accompanying conviction in the ability to communicate with the dead is also widespread.

In Ancient India, through shamanism and Yoga, the concept of a conscious entity that remains independent of the body has formed the foundation of Indian Spirituality for thousands of years. If the consciousness of the individual was weighed down as a result of Karma, then they would be born into another body. This concept remains a central tenet of Indian belief.

In ancient China, the spirits of the "ancestors" were thought to survive physical death and remain in touch with their descendents on the earth plane. These spirits were honored and revered, and often consulted for advice in daily life.

In ancient Egypt after death, the soul was ushered into the presence of Osiris (King of the Underworld). The soul of the deceased was judged in a symbolic weighing of the heart in a scale with feathers representing truth or right conduct. If the heart was dark with untruth and heavy with misdeeds then serious consequences occurred. But if the soul was light with truth and good deeds, "then a coming forth into Light" would take place — which serves to remind us of the similarity contained in the near-death experience. The Egyptians may have been the first civilized culture to embrace the belief that after death, life continues. In the final chapter of *The Egyptian Book of the Dead*, comprised of funerary texts that were recited to accompany the deceased into eternal life, the soul is deemed to be one with creation:

I am Yesterday, Today, and Tomorrow, and I have the power to be born a second time.

In ancient Greece, Pythagoras, Socrates, and Plato believed in an afterlife where good deeds were rewarded and evil-doers suffered punishment designed to eventually change their behavior. They also believed in the concept of reincarnation.

In the African religious traditions, it was believed that a Supreme Being controlled the workings of the universe, and that life did not cease at the moment of physical death but continued in another realm of existence. This transition did not change the personality of the individual, but merely heralded a change in condition. Death of the physical body was viewed to be the start of the individual's deeper spiritual connection to all of creation, and an ability to commune between the visible and invisible realms. The goal of life was deemed to be achieving the state of an ancestor, who could maintain direct contact with the earthly realms of existence after death. In the spirit world, an individual gained a new body that was identical to the previous earthly body — but endowed with enhanced abilities to communicate with those still living.

The Native American religious traditions were aimed at instilling a sense of wholeness that would unite the community and the natural world in a state of harmonious balance. In many rituals that induced altered states of consciousness, communication was established with the spirit world and the souls of the dead, who were believed to be part of the spiritual dimensions.

The three great religions of Judaism, Christianity, and Islam came to essentially share a similar belief in the transitional nature of death and the existence of an afterlife, where the virtuous are rewarded and the evil are punished. In Orthodox Judaism, the concept of resurrection of the dead is central to the cardinal values of the Jewish faith. The Christians believed that the ultimate destination of the soul was celestial paradise, and in the liturgy of Saint Basil of Alexandria, Christ is asked to lead Christian souls to a "Grassy place by quiet waters, in a luxurious park from whence pain, sadness and groaning have fled." The spiritual dimension of Islam manifests in Sufism, and reflects the inner desire of the individual to be reunited with God. Through ecstatic dance, music and poetry, the Sufi masters entered a trance-like state that resulted in transcendence of everyday consciousness, and translated the inner numinous dimensions of the *Qur'an*. Many of the Sufi poets experienced a connection to higher realities, and understood that although the physical body would perish at the moment of death, the life of the soul continued. The possibility of reincarnation was not entirely ruled out, by some of the more mystically inclined followers of these traditions.

Today, the celebration of the Day of the Dead festival is held throughout Mexico. This combines practices and rituals from the ancient Aztec and Mayan cultures with Spanish Catholic influences. The aim is to provide an opportunity to transcend the profane aspects of life and enter sacred space — in which past, present, and future merge together, lifting the veil that separates this earthly existence from other forms of consciousness. During such an event, the participants return to the mythical *illud tempus*, and enter primordial time — which never changes, and is eternal. These rituals reflect the desire to return to the source of a divine presence. A desire that seems to be inherent in all human beings.

The celebration of the Day of the Dead reflects the life of the individual as parallel to that of nature — which transcends physical death. The death and resurrection of Christ, symbolized through the ritual of the mass, illustrates once more this concept of death and resurrection. From their ancient ancestors, the Mexican people have come to view death as a transition and not an ending.

The Day of the Dead incorporates a rite of passage that follows the dynamic three-part pattern of separation, transition, and incorporation. The deceased has gone through these stages, and the point of the festival is to honor the evolution of the soul from earthly existence into an altered state of consciousness. This remembrance of the dead reminds the living that, as James Hillman points out in his book *Re-Visioning Psychology*, "it is not upon life that our ultimate individuality centers, but upon death. Its kingdom is the world under and within all life, and there souls go home." At the heart of death and rituals for the dead, there is a fundamental paradox — the living and the dead mutually sustain each other, for death is an irreversible transformation that takes place in order to ensure that consciousness continues.

Communication from the spirit world dates back to early civilization, and has a very long history. The account in the Old Testament of King Saul's contact with a spirit, through the channel of a medium, is an example of this type of phenomena. The Judaic and Christian traditions acknowledged that such contact was possible, but there was ambivalence and fear surrounding the subject that many people viewed as the work of malign forces or the devil. This was certainly the Christian viewpoint, despite the psychic abilities demonstrated by Jesus Christ — who appeared to his disciples many times during the forty days following his death, and advised his disciples and followers that they could do the same and more. In early Christian art, the eagle symbolized the figure of Christ, who acted as a psychopomp and led souls upward toward the stars.

In ancient China and Greece, a form of the modern ouija board was used to contact the dead, and this practice can be traced back as far as

2,500 years ago. Greeks who wished to interact with the spirit of deceased loved ones also visited the Oracle of the Dead at Acheron, which dates back to the beginning of the third century B.C. The building consisted of an underground chamber where Persephone (the Goddess of the Underworld) and Hades (Lord of the Dead) were believed to reside. Pilgrims would assemble and undergo a long initiation, in which they would remain isolated as they recited prayers and invocations, and partook in rituals that would prepare them to make contact with the spirits of the deceased.

Dr. Raymond Moody has recreated this ancient form of spirit communication by constructing a similar structure, in which mirrors are used to facilitate the psychic process of communication with the dead. In his book *Reunions: Visionary Encounters with Departed Loved Ones*, Moody relates how, after going through a form of initiatory preparation (that includes concentrating and sending telepathic messages to those on the other side), 85% of those studied claimed to make contact with the spirit of a deceased loved one — but the spirit contacted was not always the one they intended to contact. Although most of these meetings took place within the oracle (known as a psychomanteum), 25% of the individuals who reported successful contact also described having communication some time later in their own homes, as they awakened to see apparitions of their loved ones materializing at the end of the bed. These people also recount receiving information from the deceased — information of which they had no previous knowledge, and which later proved to be correct. In the book, Dr. Moody gives instructions for building a psychomanteum, for those interested in carrying out their own experiments.

Modern science has tended to be skeptical about the subject of after-death communication, but some scientists have pursued investigations, using scientific means to study the field of psychic phenomena and life after death. Psychical research, more recently known as Parapsychology, arose in response to the widespread popularity of Spiritualism in the second half of the nineteenth century — a time when there was popular acceptance of after-death communication.

The modern-day Spiritualist movement was founded in 1848, following the Fox family's famous communication with a departed spirit. In 1847 the Fox family, which included two young daughters, moved into a house in New York. Over the next several months, they were kept awake at night by strange and inexplicable raps and bangs. Finally, one night, the two sisters began mimicking the sounds, that were then repeated by the rapping in some form of communication. The spirit eventually identified himself, through a devised code, as the spirit of a peddler, Charles B Rosna, who had been murdered in the house. Following his instructions, the cellar was dug up and a skeleton was found. The story became a sensation in the news, and the sisters became celebrities — a role they often wished to escape from.

The core beliefs of Spiritualism are founded on the principle that there is no death and that after discarding the physical body, the spiritual or etheric body transitions into the spirit world. Spirits return to make their presence known because they have a desire to prove that their essence still exists in another form; they also want to bring love and comfort to those still on the earth plane, and communicate the interrelatedness of the material and spiritual worlds. On occasions, the spirit of a deceased person will be "stuck" in the earthly realm. This could be due to trauma at death, or a number of other possible reasons. Such an occurrence can sometimes manifest in a ghostly haunting or apparition, and often a medium can assist the spirit to let go of attachment to the physical world and move on.

A common way in which spirits communicate is through the channel of a medium who is sensitive to the vibrations of the spirit world, and so able to convey messages. These communications can manifest in a number of ways, including: clairvoyance, clairaudience, levitation, automatic writing, psychometry, voices, and materializations.

As more and more spiritualistic mediums appeared in the community at large during this period, individual scientists and a few small research teams began their own investigations. Fraudulent mediums were exposed, but some apparently genuine mediums were also discovered. Extensive testing of the medium D. D. Home, conducted by the famous chemist Sir William Crookes and other scientific researchers produced incredible displays of psychic phenomena, with no signs of detectable fraud.

By the 1800's, the scientific establishment could not ignore the challenges posed by psychical activity as spiritual communities began to flourish. In 1882, the Society for Psychical Research was founded in England, and its membership included some of the best scientific minds of the day. An American chapter was later formed.

Members of the American Society for Psychical Research, together with their British counterparts, undertook a joint research project. Their subject was Mrs. Piper, an American medium whose abilities were closely studied by prominent researchers for over forty years. Elaborate precautions were taken to exclude any possibility of fraud. Private detectives were hired by Mrs. Piper's chief investigator in America, Dr. Richard Hodgson, to follow her and see if she made any attempt to retrieve information about deceased people to use in her mediumistic messages.

Initially, Hodgson was very skeptical about a medium's ability to communicate with the spirit realms, but he later conceded that he believed there could be no other explanation, for Mrs. Piper divulged astoundingly accurate information about people of whom she had no previous knowledge. Ultimately, all of the researchers became convinced of Mrs. Piper's credibility, and compiled records of the many paranormal communications that resulted from her mediumistic trances.

However, there was some controversy as to the source of Mrs. Piper's information, and some of the investigators thought it may have been relayed through a highly developed ESP ability. Over time, and after amassing more research data on a number of seemingly genuine psychics, the ESP. hypothesis proved to be problematical to psychical researchers. In many cases, a medium would give information which was unknown to the person who was receiving the information, and a further check from another source would reveal the accuracy of the message. There were also instances of "cross-correspondences," where communications given by different mediums were specifically related to each other. It became clear that ESP. could not adequately explain the phenomena, which — investigators became convinced — represented evidence of the survival of physical death, and of communication from the "other side."

When F.W.H. Myers died in 1901, most of the founding members of the Society for Psychical Research were also deceased. It was certain that these researchers would try to communicate if this was possible, and that they would attempt something that would have evidential value. By this time the society was working with several seemingly gifted psychics besides Mrs. Piper, and messages did begin to come through.

As details from the monitored séances conducted with these mediums were analyzed for content and accuracy, it became apparent that they all related to one other in some sort of pattern. The varied references, which had come through the different mediums, only made sense as a coherent message when they were put together. None of the mediums seemed to be aware of this fact when they received their parts of the message. They were also unfamiliar with the symbolic content of the communications, as they were related in classical and poetic forms that the alleged spirits of the deceased researchers would have been completely familiar with. Myers himself had been a classicist, and received an English education that heavily emphasized the classics.

Following the death of the famous magician, Harry Houdini, in 1926, his widow offered $10,000 to any medium who could bring through the secret code which Houdini had agreed to communicate to his wife — the only other person who knew it — after his death. In 1928, the renowned medium, Arthur Ford, who served as a mediumistic channel for a great number of after-death communications, including séances conducted under the scrutiny of the Spiritual Frontiers Fellowship, relayed a message he had received from Houdini's mother. This resulted in clearing the psychic air, enabling Houdini himself to communicate. After hearing

Ford's information, Houdini's wife wrote to him and stated that, aside from "one or two trivial inaccuracies…there was nothing in the message that could be contradicted." She also added that if this information had been received while Houdini was still alive, it would have made a tremendous difference in his life. In late 1928, Ford communicated directly with Houdini, and finally the secret code came through, and was forwarded to the widow.

In her book *The Wheel of Life: A Memoir of Living and Dying,* Elisabeth Kubler-Ross relates that, after the eventual death of Mrs. Schwartz (a former patient of Kubler-Ross), she had become disillusioned with the many changes taking place in the medical world. These changes affected some aspects of her work, and she was seriously considering giving it all up. One day, she decided to advise a colleague that she would not continue with her renowned Death and Dying seminars. As Elisabeth began to speak to her associate, a woman appeared between them and hovered in the air; she seemed to be transparent, and smiled. Elisabeth explained to her colleague that she could feel this ghostly presence, who wanted to speak with her. He responded by saying that he could see nothing, and then made a rapid exit. As soon as he left, the apparition approached Elisabeth, and told her that she had returned to tell her something. For a second, Elisabeth believed that she might be experiencing hallucinations from the results of the extreme stress she had been under, but she followed the woman into the office and immediately recognized her as being Mrs. Schwartz.

Although she had died ten months earlier, Mrs. Schwartz appeared as her normal self. She told Elisabeth that she had returned to thank her for everything that she had done for her in life, and to persuade her to continue her work in the field of death and dying.

Elisabeth was stunned, and wondered how on earth Mrs. Schwartz could have had any idea that she was planning to resign. Mrs. Schwartz emphasized that Elisabeth would receive help from the spirit world to continue her work, and asked her if she could hear her message. Elisabeth replied that she could. She then asked for proof that Mrs. Schwartz was really present in the room, asking her to write a note for a Reverend Gaines, who had also helped Mrs. Schwartz while she was alive. The ghostly presence accepted a sheet of paper and a pen, and scribbled a few lines before vanishing.

Following this after-death communication, Elisabeth gave up all thoughts of quitting her job. In fact, she returned home feeling energized and optimistic about the future, convinced without a shadow of doubt that Mrs. Schwartz had appeared to her from the spirit world to prevent her from making the wrong decision about her work.

This communication from Mrs. Schwartz firmly reiterated Elisabeth's belief that if a person were open to the possibility, they could have a genuine transcendent spiritual or mystical vision that would connect them to proof of an afterlife.

In July of 2006, Victor Zammit, a lawyer who has conducted extensive research into the case for the afterlife, reported on a séance that took place in Sydney, Australia, with materialization medium, David Thompson. The nine sitters were all professional people, and the séance was conducted under the most stringent conditions, in which the medium was strapped to his chair to avoid any possible kind of fraud.

Zammit claims that during this séance, all of the participants felt an abnormal coldness around their legs and feet, and witnessed the materialization of several spirits. These included that of Sir Arthur Conan Doyle, who gave a talk on survival after death, and what one experiences. At one point, this entity approached Zammit and shook his hand, which felt warm and solid. The spirit-hand was described as being huge, twice the size of the hand of the medium. At the end of the sitting, all of the security precautions remained fully intact, and Zammit later commented, "While there was no attempt to validate the identity of the materialized etherics, I am one-hundred percent convinced that paranormal activity did take place."

In a 1993 survey conducted by The National Opinion Research Center, four out of every ten people interviewed reported some form of after-death communication. In a 1994 Gallup Poll, 49% of individuals questioned stated that they were open to the concept of this type of phenomenon taking place. In the book *Love Beyond Life*, Joel Martin and Patricia Romanowski have compiled many accounts of after-death communications. Their research "suggests that it is very likely people have many more direct communication experiences than they realize." In 1987, Father Andrew Greeley, a Roman Catholic priest and author, carried out his own investigation — and discovered that 42% of Americans purported to have experienced communication with the dead. This form of communication can occur in various ways, such as experiencing the presence of a loved one, smelling their perfume or scent, or becoming aware of subtle messages indicating that the spirit of the deceased is still around.

Reports of the spirit or essence of a deceased person appearing as a "ghost" date back into the pre-Christian era, and one of the earliest sightings was recorded by Pliny The Younger (63 -113 AD). He relates that an early philosopher, Athenodoros Cananities, stayed at a house in Athens that was said to be haunted. During the night, Athenodoros saw an apparition of an old man whose hands and feet were shackled by chains. The spirit motioned to the philosopher to follow him, but the ghost soon disappeared. Later, a dig was carried out in the spot where the old man had vanished, and his bones and the shackles were exposed. After a proper burial, the ghostly presence was never seen again. In Greek mythology, Odysseus journeyed through Hades, and encountered the ghosts or "shades" of many of his former comrades, even though he didn't know that some of them had died.

Many similar sightings have been recorded throughout the world. Some of the most famous are the various ghostly apparitions of historical figures that were imprisoned in the Tower of London. These include the headless figures of Anne Boleyn and Thomas A. Becket. Biggin Hill, a former airbase in World War II, is said to be one of the most haunted places in England. In the USA, many people have claimed to see or sense the presence of Abraham Lincoln, a former President who still supposedly resides in the White House.

One of the most common forms of after-death communication can be experienced in the dreaming state. This is attributed to the fact that when sleeping, we enter an altered state of consciousness that enables us to become far more receptive to the spirit world, as our everyday fears and defenses regarding this type of manifestation are bypassed. In many indigenous cultures and ancient world philosophies, the astral body is believed to separate from the physical being in the dreaming state, resulting in an out-of-body experience during which it is possible to meet with departed spirits.

After-death communications that occur while in the dreaming state have a remarkable quality, and clearly stand out as being different from the ordinary dream. They have a numinous translucent energy, and are extremely vivid, in both color and essence. The deceased appears with a vibrant energy, and is frequently shown to be young and in perfect health. Often, the messages they convey assure the individual that they are in direct communication with the spirit of the dead person. These dreams are so striking that they retain their initial impact and imagery. In this type of after-death communication, it is possible to have a direct conversation with a loved one, and to even exchange a warm embrace. The resulting sense of well-being and inner peace, after experiencing such an event, affirms the connectedness of all beings and serves as a reminder that life does not cease at the moment of physical death.

The British and American Societies for Psychical Research have continued to amass an increasingly impressive amount of data pertaining to the possibility of survival beyond death, and the nature of the afterlife. Over the years, they have worked with several extraordinary mediums. Contemporary psychical research has also added to the weight of scientific data related to the probability of survival after death. The number of scientific researchers in the field of parapsychology has steadily increased over the years, as has the number of institutions sponsoring their work.

Private organizations and major universities are involved in a variety of research projects aimed at addressing the question of the continuation of consciousness after death.

Research into out-of-body experiences has been conducted for many years, British geologist, Dr. Robert Crookall, collected and analyzed hundreds of OBEs, and his findings led him to concur that a release of consciousness from the body did occur during these experiences, in an "apparitional" form that could survive death.

Further research was undertaken by Dr. Charles Tart and also Dr. William Dement, a well-known authority on sleep research, Dement could not classify such occurrences as either sleeping or waking states, for subjects were able to report in an accurate manner on what they could observe at target areas inaccessible from their physical locations during the experiments. There is now much research data indicating the validity of OBEs, which proves to be an experience that is strikingly similar to the "magical flight, "bird soul," and "astral body" descriptions found in shamanic and mystical traditions.

A tenet of belief for thousands of years in India and other parts of Asia is the concept of reincarnation or rebirth. In contrast to the main traditions of Egyptian religion, Judaism, Christianity and Islam, the religious traditions of India and Tibet do not envision an after-death state of an unchanging and eternal nature. A life review and reckoning is recorded in the sacred literature of Hinduism, but after a certain period, the individual is reborn into this world again, unless they have been liberated from Karma. The following quotation from the Upanishhads describes this process:

He who lacks discrimination, whose mind is unsteady and whose heart is impure never reaches the goal, but is born again and again. But he who has discrimination, whose mind is steady and whose heart is pure, reached the goal, and having reached it is born no more (*Katha Upanishad* 5).

This goal of escape from the continuous cycle of birth, death, and rebirth has been the preoccupation of Hinduism and Buddhism. The attainment of liberation takes the individual beyond all realms of conditioned phenomenal existence, and is considered as a path open to all and leading to a goal we can all eventually attain. This concept of reincarnation is not confined to Asian religions, but is also prevalent in many other cultures.

Intensive parapsychological research in this area did not begin until the 1960's. Some studies were conducted in France and England at the end of the nineteenth century, but there was little scientific interest in the subject, despite its obvious relationship to survival after death. This changed when Dr. Ian Stevenson published the book *Twenty Cases Suggestive of Reincarnation*. He subsequently compiled reports assembled from experiences in Virginia, Beirut, and areas of India. The purpose of this study was to reassess cases of children who seemed to remember past lives. He was accompanied by Tom Shroder, a veteran journalist and editor of the *Washington Post*. The findings were published in the book *Old Souls: Compelling Evidence from Children Who Remember Past Lives*. Shroder began the trip as a skeptical journalist, but ended up convinced by concrete evidence he could not discount. He's now certain that he encountered an authentic phenomenon, and a scrupulously honest researcher.

Reincarnated children from various cultures and countries usually offer corroborative information regarding their previous lives — sometimes in incredible detail. Much of this data has been examined meticulously, and confirms both the children's stories and their inexplicable knowledge of a prior incarnation. The children usually stop speaking of their past lives as they grow older, and these memories slip into their unconscious minds.

Supporting evidence to support the belief in an afterlife can be found in the many reports of deathbed visions. Numerous hospice workers have become very familiar with this phenomenon, which is a powerful, calming, and reassuring experience that the dying can encounter immediately prior to death. The apparitions that appear to people approaching death are often those of deceased relatives, but they can materialize in the form of a divine being such as an angel, and they manifest to escort the dying person in their transition from this world to the next.

Such occurrences can be traced back through history, and the passage of the soul from an earthly plane of existence to the eternal continuum of consciousness is well documented in many of the world's religions. In indigenous cultures, it is often the shaman traveling between the lands of the living and the dead, who accompanies the dying. In Greek mythology it was Hermes, the god of travel, who acted as a psychopomp and led the dying souls on to their final resting place. In the Christian tradition, there are legends from the third century that detail how Christ appeared to the Virgin Mary to announce the hour of her death and accompany her into the heavenly realms. In the thirteenth century, Caesarius of Heisterbach, a German monk, recounted many such incidents in a *Dialogue of Miracles.*

Early studies into deathbed visions were undertaken by Dr. James Hyslop of Columbia University, and Sir William F. Barrett of Dublin University. Their main area of interest involved cases in which a dying person was visited at the hour of death — by a dead relative or friend whom the dying person believed to be still among the living.

Further research into the phenomenon took place during the 1960s, and was conducted by Dr. Karlis Osis, who later published his finding in *Deathbed Observations of Physicians and Nurses.* During this study, he analyzed the results of questionnaires completed by doctors and nurses, who had attended more than 35,000 deaths. Osis termed deathbed apparitions as hallucinations, because they could not be scientifically substantiated, but the results of his study nevertheless substantiated the findings of previous researchers — verifying that dying people who experience these visions usually see a deceased family member or loved one, and that the loved ones are making their presence known in order to accompany the dying person on their journey to the afterlife.

With the help of Dr. Erlandur Haraldsson, Osis carried out further research among doctors and nurses in the United States and northern India. This research confirmed the results of his earlier studies; the only difference was that in India, the dying person was more likely to see the apparition of a religious figure.

Often these types of experiences are dismissed as hallucinations caused by medications or a shortage of oxygen to the brain. However, this kind of phenomenon has been recorded among numerous people who have not been on any type of medication, and who have been coherent as death approached. There are also many instances of individuals who have encountered these visitors from other realms in dreams and visions, several weeks prior to their death and the dying process.

Following her many years of working with the dying and their families, Elisabeth Kubler-Ross gathered numerous accounts of the phenomenon of deathbed visions. These not only further affirmed her belief in an afterlife, but also assured her that no one dies alone, and that there are always spirit guides who are ready to appear to escort the dying person in their transition.

Many people involved in death and dying have had similar experiences, in which a person who is just about to make their transition will appear to them in a vision or dream. In some cases, the individual has no prior knowledge that the person is in the dying process, but experiences a sudden moment of "knowing" that the person has died, which is later verified to be correct.

Present-day research into this type of occurrence — which is still viewed as a controversial subject by some members of the scientific world who remain unconvinced of life after death — is now being carried out by a multinational team of doctors, nurses, and neuroscientists that includes Dr. Peter Fenwick, a British neuropsychiatrist. A recent report in the *American Journal of Hospice and Palliative Medicine* (published in the early part of 2006, and co-authored by Dr. Fenwick) featured a survey carried out among nurses, doctors, and palliative caregivers who had all been present many times in the forty-eight hours immediately preceding death. All had either been told of a deathbed vision by a patient, or had personally experienced the phenomenon. They all remained convinced that such occurrences are an integral and natural part of the dying process.

Many scientists argue that deathbed visions are projections of the dying brain to ease the ordeal of facing physical death, and that the similar visions often experienced by medical staff, or friends and family of a dying person can be attributed to stress, or fear of losing a loved one. However, Dr. Fenwick does not believe that this hypothesis satisfactorily explains the many recorded instances of this type of event taking place. He suggests the possibility of the dying person having the capability to transcend everyday consciousness and communicate directly with the spiritual realms of existence — an ability that is not yet fully understood.

A great number of people who have been with a dying person also report instances of a radiant light surrounding the body of the dying person, as their soul detaches from the physical body. Reuben Beckham, an NDE survivor featured in an earlier story, works in hospice as a spiritual counselor to the dying. He describes this phenomenon as a type of "aura" that is seen floating above the dying person.

Although there is often a reluctance to discuss such incidents, both the dying and the living who experience this type of event have a numinous, sacred experience, which does much to further support evidence of an afterlife, and provides the individual with an opportunity to reevaluate the concept that consciousness ceases to exist at the moment of death.

For many people, the power of prayer also offers the individual a method of engaging in direct communication with a higher power. Although prayer is normally associated with religious ceremonies, prayer in its essence, remains an act through which any individual, whether or not possessed of religious convictions, can enter a state in which the barriers of linear time and space are transcended. In this state that has many similarities to meditation, it is possible to gain an awareness of eternity; and time, as we perceive it, seems to stand still. In his book

Prayer is Good Medicine, Larry Dossey discusses the impact that the power of prayer can have on our understanding of death and dying. He asks:

> Is life destined to end tragically in death? It depends on the answers we give to the nature of time. If time doesn't flow as we assume, perhaps we should take another look at the meaning of death. This is not to suggest that death does not happen but that its significance may be different from what we ordinarily assume.
>
> It may not be the absolute ending we think it is.
>
> How can we decide? Instead of praying not to die, perhaps we might pray for a different understanding of time – time as an eternity instead of a flowing process always pointing towards annihilation...Prayer can reveal what eternity feels like. For those who have gained this awareness, immortality is not a theoretical possibility but a certainty.

Certainly, the power of prayer seems to provide a way for human beings to gain direct access to this higher source. The recital of Christian prayers, or mantras from the Eastern traditions, can instill the individual with a sense of the connectedness to all their fellow beings, and to something greater and more powerful than the self. Prayer provides the individual with the ability to intercede with this higher power for the well-being of both the living and the dead. Distant healing through prayer, which has been rigorously tested under laboratory conditions, appears to work — and provides another example of the ability to transcend our perceived human limitations.

Many parapsychologists, who have gathered extensive data in all of these areas of psychical research, acknowledge the very strong mass of evidence suggesting the survival of bodily death, and a subsequent afterlife. However, controversy still rages in the scientific community on the validity of parapsychological research, even though telepathy and psychokinesis have been scientifically proven to exist.

Perhaps undeniable proof of a continuum of consciousness after physical death is not far behind. The constantly-growing number of researchers around the world continues to expand a diverse and extensive data base. It may one day be possible to access solid, undeniable scientific evidence that will prove the age-old beliefs of survival, and enable these beliefs to become an accepted part of modern-day life. For it appears that all interactions with death and dying, and all communications from the afterlife, seem to trigger a memory of a long-forgotten wisdom, and a yearning to return to the source of the light.

As Plato relates in the *Phaedo*, when Socrates was about to drink the poison hemlock and bid farewell to earthly existence, he suffered no fear or regret, for he was certain of his ultimate glorious destination, and he felt only compassion for his misguided and ignorant executioners. His last prayer was, "I may and must ask the gods to prosper my journey from this to the other world – even so – and so be it according to my prayers."

If we choose to live our lives as a practice of conscious living and dying, we — like Socrates — can eliminate the fear of death, because we will come to the realization that <u>death</u> heralds the beginning of new <u>life</u>.

JOHN'S STORY

Souls are always hastening to the upper world where they desire
to dwell
Socrates

From an early age, John firmly believed in the concept of an afterlife. He knew that his mother, Rose, would be an ideal candidate for communication from the spirit world. They had many conversations about the possibility prior to her death, and she had promised to make her presence known to him and his daughter, if such a thing were possible. He was not surprised when Rose managed to keep this promise – as he began to receive subtle messages from his mother in the months following her transition.

The beautiful town of Ojai, California, is imbued with a fine cultural heritage. Evidence suggests that early indigenous cultures inhabited the land as much as 25,000 years ago. Starting about 3,000 years ago, and lasting into the late eighteenth century, Ojai was home to the Chumash Indians. The name itself is a Spanish version of a Chumash Indian word meaning "moon," or perhaps "nest of the moon." But within fifty years, these Native American tribes were decimated through starvation and disease as Spanish invaders tried to "civilize" and convert the Chumash to Christianity. Nevertheless, the sacred presence of these early ancestors is preserved and experienced in the land where they hunted, harvested crops, built boats, and produced beautiful rock art.

Surrounded by majestic mountains, Ojai became famous for its scenery, climate, natural hot springs and serenity, and gained a reputation as a place of natural healing. The valley is home to massive oak trees, some of which are hundreds of years old and all species of wildlife have settled in the surrounding landscape. Known for its *pink moment* sunsets when the spectacular Topa Topa mountains are flooded with a luminous rosy tint, Ojai featured in the Frank Capra movie *Lost Horizon*, in the scene where the travelers come upon the inspiring landscape of the hidden Himalayan valley of *Shangri-La*. The Ojai valley provides the perfect setting to become at one with nature and experience the interconnectedness of all beings. It was the ideal place for John's mother, Rose, to spend her final months because, although bedridden, life never failed to stimulate, amuse or engage her, even from the supposed confines of her bedroom window.

* * * * *

John

I don't recall ever having a fear of death and remember that even as a young child, I felt pretty philosophical about the death of my beloved grandmother. But, my understanding and acceptance of the dying process deepened as I became interested and involved in psychic research and parapsychology.

When I was attending College, I had a deep-rooted desire to experience Asian culture, and to study either Kung Fu or Karate. At the time, martial arts were little known in America, and there were few master teachers to study with. I focused my attention on how I might achieve this aim, and was delighted when my positive intentions presented me with the opportunity to live and study in Japan as a cultural exchange student.

At one of the first welcoming dinners in Japan, I was seated directly across from a notable gentleman, who gained my attention through his remarkable presence even though I hadn't actually spoken to him. Looking back, I see how the whole seemingly random sequence of events was part of a pattern, which Dr. Carl Jung referred to as synchronicity. The gentlemen was introduced as a renowned master of both Karate-Do (the Way of the Empty Hand), and Kendo (the Way of the Sword). He knew of my profound interest in Japanese martial arts, and invited me to visit his dojo to experience the practice of traditional Karate-Do, which was the very art to which I was longing to commit myself. Although I was also able to meet and study with other masters, I devoted myself to Master Ujita and his teachings. I heard stories of paranormal activities connected to the martial arts, and had several experiences of my own during this period.

An intuitive, interconnected state of mind known as *Mushin no Shin*, translated to mean "mind of no-mind," is the state of consciousness in which the highest expression of the martial arts unfolds. I was able to access this state, although only intermittently. When I later studied Chinese internal martial arts and QiGong, I learned even more about the mysterious but accessible intrinsic bio-energy known as Prana, Ki, and Qi/Chi. Some Asian masters of martial arts have accomplished extraordinary paranormal feats, and the types of psychic abilities that are understood and researched in clinical parapsychology. This period of study was my introduction into the world of Psi, and Eastern parapsychology.

Some years later, after returning to California, I opened my first Karate school. I started to seriously study parapsychology and related subjects. In the late 1960's, a student of mine named Bob, told me about a psychic called Rosalee. She was reputed to have genuine psychic abilities, and was able to give specific information about matters of which she had no previous knowledge. Bob had taken a reading with Rosalee. She was amazingly accurate, though she did seem to mistakenly name one of his deceased relatives when the woman was readily identifiable. But when Bob told his mother about what had happened and the use of the "wrong" name, she was able to confirm that it was a family childhood nickname that he had never heard. The use of this unfamiliar name made the after-death communication all the more credible. After hearing of other people's similar stories, I decided to consult Rosalee myself.

I was ushered into Rosalee's home. We sat at a table and she began her reading. She noted my interest in parapsychology, and said, "You will soon be moving to a coastal town in California with "San" as part of the name." She couldn't give any more specific information, but added, "I can see the beach and the ocean, and when you move to this city, you will become involved with organizations and institutions that are connected with..." As she uttered these words, she paused, because psychic was not the right term, nor was parapsychology, even though the field she was describing encompassed both terms. She also described a spiritual and educational aspect to the subject matter that I would become involved with.

Some time later, I found myself moving to the beautiful coastal city of Santa Barbara, California. This move hadn't been in my plans when I consulted Rosalee, and I soon became immersed in psychical activities, just as she predicted. For a while, I worked for a private foundation where I arranged lectures, seminars and workshops on topics related to parapsychology. These lectures featured some of the veteran researchers in the field. Then I became involved with teaching and coordinating parapsychology courses at the University of Santa Barbara Extension.

Later, my work in this field led me to discover Ojai, where I now live. It's a small town nestled in a mountain valley, and renowned as a haven of tranquility.

Years ago, I was driving the short distance from Santa Barbara to Ojai several times a week to study parapsychology with Dr. Laurence Bendit, a British psychiatrist and parapsychologist, who was living there. During my commute, I would pass by a stately home next to the 101 freeway and just south of Santa Barbara, in Summerland. I learned from Dr Bendit that a spiritual colony had been founded there in the late 1800's. I felt strangely drawn to the house, and Dr. Bendit surmised that it might have been a site for Spiritualist séances that took place in the heyday of the community and that perhaps some psychic residue, or the traces of a haunting, might remain. Since we were immersed in the study of parapsychology, he didn't consider it unusual that I might feel a psychic pull to the building. It was soon turned into a restaurant called "The Big Yellow House," and now it was open to the public, so I could go there whenever

I liked.

One evening, I had dinner at the restaurant with my wife, mother, and friend, Bob Mayfield, who was working at a Santa Barbara research and development company. When the waitress came to take our order, I asked her, "Do you know if there have been any ghostly sightings or unexplained paranormal happenings taking place in the building?" She looked at me, and excitedly replied, "Yes." She then recounted how members of the staff and the manager had experienced strange things in the house. Heavy stainless steel vats placed on the kitchen floor, used to whip up the large amounts of butter to be served with the restaurant's famous cornbread, seemed to have taken on a life of their own. The kitchen staff reported that they seemed to careen across the floor, reminding them of something out of *The Sorcerer's Apprentice* in Walt Disney's *Fantasia*.

However, it seemed that one room in particular was the focal point, in which a strange presence seemed to reside. There was an inexplicable coldness that was felt in this area, no matter what the temperature was in the rest of the house. Waitresses that I talked to claimed that guests often asked to be seated elsewhere, and that tips were always a lot smaller when working these tables.

As we finished our meal and were leaving the restaurant, I mentioned to Bob that it might be worthwhile contacting Elizabeth Huffer, a local mediumistic psychic with a solid reputation, whom we'd both met. Then, in the parking lot, I glanced back at the house and stopped in stunned amazement. There, framed in the second story window, stood Elizabeth! Bob recognized her as well, and we both quickly returned to the restaurant and went upstairs to the second floor.

We brought Elizabeth into the target room and asked her to see what she could pick up. After quietly tuning in, she motioned to us, and we left the area to the few diners who were watching us curiously. Elizabeth told us that she had "seen" a huge black man conducting a ritual attended by other spirits. She was able to communicate with him, and urge him and the others to move on into the higher regions of Light in the afterlife. The spirit group acknowledged her message, but showed little interest in it. Still she hoped her advice might have some effect.

We said goodbye to Elizabeth and her husband, and left by way of the gift shop. I felt prompted to ask the young man behind the counter if he knew anything about what had happened, and said, "Do you know anything about a giant black man that supposedly haunts the building?"

He replied, "Yes I do, and I'm presently compiling a history of the house, which has a remarkable background."

He went on to explain that the Big Yellow House had originally been built as a home in the late nineteenth century by a Mr. H.L. Williams, the founder of Summerland, and it had been a focal point for spiritual séances. One of the practicing mediums was called Harry Allen, and he used a unique and rather bizarre technique to access the trance-like state of consciousness required for spirit communication: he drank himself into a stupor and then passed out. The spirit that then possessed him was described as a huge black man, around seven feet tall.

On one occasion, when someone asked Allen if he could provide any physical evidence of the purported size of the spirit, he immediately felt an unseen hand closing round his head. The hand was so large that it touched the top of one of his ears, and stretched round to the other side of his face.

All the accounts of this strange spirit seemed to resonate with the presence that Elizabeth had encountered. As far as Bob and I knew, she had no knowledge of Harry Allen and his spirit giant's connection to the house, as Rod Lathim — the young man who was conducting the research — had not yet published his findings. We also had confidence in Elizabeth's genuine psychic abilities.

Eventually, Rod Lathim's book *The Spirit of the Big Yellow House* was published, and I purchased a copy and read that he mentioned an anonymous psychic (Elizabeth Huffer) and her encounter with the spirit in the upstairs room.

Following our experience with the spirit of the black giant through Elizabeth, and after listening to the various accounts of paranormal happenings from the staff, we seriously considered carrying out a scientific study of what seemed a genuine spirit haunt. It could have been possible to do this through friends at the University of California, Santa Barbara, but a busy restaurant is not really conducive to this type of research, even if permission had been granted, and so we were left with the tantalizing nature of the encounter itself.

Subsequently, I had lunch in the restaurant in the Spring of 1999; it had been remodeled and substantially changed. While visiting the gift shop, I decided to buy an updated copy of Lathim's book and was surprised to see there was no longer any mention of Elizabeth or her spirit experience.

I called Ron Lathim sometime later, and asked, "Is there any reason why the reference to my experience with Elizabeth Huffer is missing from your updated version of the book?" He went to look at his own copy and said, "I didn't intentionally remove it; this must have happened in the publishing set-up."

Then I asked him, "What effect did the experience at the Big Yellow House have on you?" He replied, "Well after this experience my own psychic abilities evolved and opened up. I was feeling uneasy about this development for some time, but now have come to value it, and see how helpful it is to others." He added, "I now feel much more comfortable with accepting the concept of physical death as well."

Here in the Ojai Valley, there have been a number of local hauntings reported over the years. A veteran psychic investigator who has written extensively on the subject and lives close to the area, claims to have seen an apparition himself while taking his class from a nearby community college on a field trip to a reputedly haunted Ojai house built in 1915. Five members of the class also saw the female apparition and verified her appearance, which included details of the old-fashioned dress she wore. They also felt a pronounced drop in temperature.

There are many recorded sightings in the area, and I think the instances of this type of phenomena taking place serve to remind us that the dead can still communicate with the living, and act as an important reminder of evidence of an afterlife.

My mother, Rose Griffin, had a great interest in life after death, and it was often a topic of discussion between us. She also liked to watch the TV programs featuring the well-known psychic mediums. One day when we were watching a John Edward show, she suddenly said to me, "You're going to find the ring Uncle Fred gave you." The ring she referred to was one that had belonged to my uncle; he'd given it to me shortly before his death to serve as a keepsake. It was a beautiful ring with an engraved tiger's eye stone, but I'd taken it off one day and subsequently lost it. It had been missing for months, even though I'd searched high and low to find it.

My mother seemed so sure that the ring would now resurface that I couldn't help but exclaim, "Do you really think you're getting messages from Uncle Fred in the way that John Edward does?" She just smiled. So, I added, "And when do you think this will happen?" She replied confidently, "Very soon." I had always known that my mother was psychic, so I didn't dismiss her prediction. That evening, I was reorganizing some furniture and, in the process, had removed a drawer from a chest and placed it on top of a stack of books. Accidentally, I tipped it over and one single item fell out and landed at my feet. I was stunned to see that it was the ring!

Since my mother had this psychic gift during her earthly life, I thought that it was highly likely that she would be able to manifest these abilities following her transition, for the afterlife is probably a low-entropy dimension where these psychic energies can manifest more easily than in our high-entropy, materially driven world. And there is excellent evidence to support the theory that these energies can cross the threshold that divides us.

My mother was known for her strong willpower, and had overcome many obstacles in her life. During World War II, she had become a supervisor in a defense plant, which was quite an achievement for a woman in those days. Later, she also had a career in the oil industry, where her hard work and determination enabled her to reach managerial status. In a predominately man's world, that took a lot of doing.

All things considered, she was an ideal candidate for after-death communication, and prior to her transition had promised to contact me and my daughter, if at all possible. She was convinced that she would be able to do so, and I believed her. When someone like my mother dies — having strong bonds with surviving loved ones, and having over her lifetime developed a deep spiritual belief in the afterlife — an after-death communication is not only more strongly indicated, but even expected. There was a poignant case which happened locally some years ago, reported by Tom Verdin in his article, *Daughter finds message in recovery of dad's ring.*

In this article, Verdin describes how on January 31, 2000, Alaska Airlines, Flight 261, plunged into the Pacific Ocean near Ventura and Santa Barbara, California. All aboard were killed, including the parents of Tracy Knizek. Tracy's father, Bob Williams, was a retired Air Force Colonel and a Grand Master Mason. He had a close relationship with his daughter and two grandchildren who lived in a house on his nine-acre property in rural Washington State. As a Grand Master Mason, Bob wore a distinctive Masonic ring which, as stated in a letter to be opened upon his death, he left to one of Tracy's brothers. Tracy and her father had made an agreement in which they promised that whoever died first would, "let the other person know its okay, like we think it's going to be." Tracy had reminded her father of this agreement when her grandfather died, just a year prior to his own death.

Following the crash, efforts were undertaken to recover wreckage from the ocean. A commercial fisherman, who took part in the search, found an unusual and quite distinctive item in the debris. It was the Grand Master Mason ring that Bob always wore. The ring was not discovered until the crash remains covering the deck of the 32-foot boat had been unloaded and turned over to investigators. In the process of cleaning jet fuel off the boat decks, the ring was discovered, "nestled in the notched handle of a deck hatch." The boat owner, Scott Jarvis, stated in an Associated Press article that appeared in the February 4, 2000 edition of the Santa Barbara News-Press, how the fact that the ring had, "landed on floating debris after the crash, that it stayed on deck despite choppy seas and wasn't lost in the mass of debris dumped on the shore was almost unbelievable... It's like he sent it from heaven and just set it on the boat." A photograph of the ring was featured in the article.

As a career military officer, it's easy to see that Bob would have had a well-developed sense of purpose that would have been reinforced by the Masonic tradition and belief in the continuum of consciousness and its rituals of transformation, regeneration, and resurrection to a higher state of being. This would have made him an ideal candidate for after-death communication, and what more appropriate sign could he send than the ring, which was so much a part of him and symbolized his philosophy on life?

Through my perspective on death and the afterlife, I felt that my mother's death was a release from the confines of her failing health and increasing dementia. I had also been concerned because I had injured my back lifting her passive weight, and had found it more and more difficult to care for her at home. I had taken a leave of absence from work and the toll of caring for my mother for the six months prior to her death had left me physically, emotionally, and mentally exhausted. But, I knew that her peaceful passing in familiar surroundings with her family took her beyond the suffering of a ravaged ninety-year-old body.

Shortly after her death, I had a dream that seemed to signify a dramatic restoration of my health and vitality. In this dream, I was looking at myself in a mirror, and I was amazed at how much better shape I was in. The hair on top of my head had become much thicker, and was restored to a dark lustre. I took this as a good omen and as confirmation of my decision to seek out a high level Qigong (Chinese Yoga) master teacher. I knew that even though I accepted my mother's death, and viewed it as a welcome release for her, there were still the natural and inevitable human emotions of loss and grief. Even though I had been physically and emotionally drained through being my mother's caregiver, a Chinese traditional medical doctor diagnosed weakening of the kidneys that could affect the color and sheen of the hair. Later, my Qigong master from China, confirmed this diagnosis.

It was comforting to me and my daughter to communicate with my mother in spirit, through dreams and incidents that I believe were genuine after-death communications.

A couple of months after my mother's death, I awoke from a vivid, lucid dream, and could still hear the words of the song "What a Wonderful World" by Louis Armstrong that had featured strongly in the dream, reverberating in my mind. I had not been a fan of this particular artist, but my mother loved him and this was one of her favorite songs, but it was not one that would tend to come to mind for me, and I hadn't heard it for many years.

The dream was centered on the experience of the song and a feeling of pure, unconditional love. I once more felt my mother's loving, maternal presence, although I don't recall seeing her distinct form. I felt like a much-loved child again, enveloped in her love. At the end of the song, and in the dream, I realized that an emphasis was placed on the words, "I love you." These words occur in the middle of the song and I thought they were out of sequence, but my mother informed me telepathically that this version was especially altered to highlight these words. Then she gave me a loving kiss. I realized that she was using the medium of a favorite melody to let me know that she was fine and blessed in her wonderful, new world, and wanted me to know that she loved me more unconditionally than ever. Needless to say, this is now also one of my most cherished songs.

Within a few months of her death, there were three instances that all showed signs of further communications from my mother. They involved the appearance of different creatures with which my mother had an affinity; these included a butterfly, a squirrel and wild birds. They would have been obvious choices to relay her messages.

My mother died in July, and one day in August, I received an email from my daughter telling me that she had also experienced her own love-infused dream of Rose. That afternoon I met with Annamaria to do some work on the book. As we sat at the dining room table, I noticed through the bay window that a white butterfly was darting by. I told Annamaria how white butterflies always reminded me of my mother, and she replied, "My mother also really loved butterflies, especially Monarchs; in fact she had a beautiful butterfly broach made of semi-precious stones that I keep on a little altar in my bedroom in honor of her memory." Just as she finished speaking, our attention was drawn to a large Monarch butterfly that we could see flying in a straight line right in front of us. We couldn't have wished for a better symbol that related to both of our mothers at that moment. I recalled the last verse of a poem that my mother had written about butterflies, which seemed so appropriate:

They truly bless me with their presence
 Although I cannot tell them so
Yet, I feel that we're connected
And my thoughts, they somehow know.

The famous psychiatrist and pioneer in the field of death and dying, Dr. Elisabeth Kubler-Ross, was particularly fond of the image of a butterfly. She used it as a metaphor to illustrate the dying person's consciousness being liberated from the confining cocoon of the body at the moment of death, and freed to fly in its full glory, for the butterfly symbolizes the unconscious attraction of the soul towards the light.

When we first moved to Ojai, my mother was highly amused by the tricks of a squirrel that would perform a high-wire act, in which it scampered along a telephone line that ran near a tree, where it lived in the park behind our house. I'd also seen the squirrel many times, and its antics were a topic of conversation between us, because my mother really enjoyed reveling in the sounds and sights of nature that took place right on her doorstep.

Shortly after the butterfly episode, I was again in the dining room and my attention was caught by a squirrel on top of the neighbor's fence; it was in the throes of performing antics like no squirrel I had ever seen before. It was dancing, shaking, flipping and vibrating its tail, in what reminded me of an ecstatic Sufi dance. This went on for some considerable time, before it jumped down from the fence and disappeared. Some people could put this down to mere coincidence, but it fit the pattern of an after-death communication, because once more, it was easily recognizable as a symbol my mother would have chosen to catch my attention.

My experience with the "kissing bird" took place the following November; it was just one day prior to the four-month anniversary of my mother's death, and also happened to be the Roman Catholic observance of All Soul's Day. I was on the side patio watering some plants and there was a soft flutter of wings, as a fairly large wild bird landed on my shoulder. It looked identical to one of the birds on the illustrated chart that I had given my mother when she was bedridden and spent her days watching the birds that came to the feeder that I had placed outside her bedroom window.

I recognized the bird to be a warbler, one of her favorites that had regularly visited. It stayed with me, and I asked, "Are you my mother's spirit come to visit?" It appeared to reply in an affirmative manner, as it gave me several pecks on the cheek that felt like gentle kisses. I walked into the garage to get some bird seed, which it then proceeded to eat out of my hand. Finally, it made a chirping sound, as if saying goodbye, and flew off eastwards.

As I thought about this synchronistic occurrence, I suddenly remembered another bird connection, which hadn't dawned on me immediately.

My mother had chosen to be cremated and so my daughter Erin and I had chosen a classically graceful Chinese cloissone urn to hold her ashes that had a beautifully colored bird flying amongst exquisite flowers.

Some days later, I was out in the front of the house, when a wild warbler again swooped down and landed on the bush next to me. It was slightly different from the first bird, as the crown of its head was a tan-taupe color. It looked me straight in the eye and then landed by my feet and circled around me before flying off. The chances of two obviously wild birds displaying the same kind of behavior made me very aware of the fact that these happenings could be further visitations from my mother.

In the next few days, another warbler appeared when I was fixing up a new feeder. It too landed on my shoulder, and when I asked again if it was my mother, I received more kiss-like pecks on my right cheek. It stayed a while and then with some loud cries took off into the sky and disappeared from view. I firmly believe that the practice of my Qigong exercises that included meditative techniques, breathing, and movement were balancing my Qi energy and helped put me in a particularly sensitive and receptive state, which is much more open to these subtle and spiritually based manifestations.

* * * * *

All these occurrences that took place in the months following the death of John's mother made perfect sense to him, and left him with a deep sense of confirmation that although our dimensional localities and our forms may change there is continuity and connectedness that remains intact, especially when the love bond is so strong.

ANDY, KEITH AND

FRANCESCA'S STORY

How can you prove whether at this moment we are sleeping, and all our
thoughts are a dream; or whether we are awake, and talking to one
another in the waking state?

Plato

Following a near-death experience in 1986, Andy Lakey was given a
mission to create 2,000 angel paintings by the year 2000. He did as he
was instructed, and subsequently discovered that his art acted as a portal
to the spirit world. For when people touched his paintings, something
surprising happened; they made contact and received messages from
deceased relatives and friends.

It's a bright February morning and the sea air is crisp and invigorating in
Main Street, Ventura, a coastal town in southern California, where a line
of thrift stores sell secondhand clothes and discarded appliances. Across
the street, the homeless push their pitifully few belongings in shopping
carts and rummage through trash cans. In contrast, the next couple of
blocks are home to newly-planted palm trees, and it's possible to detect
delicious aromas coming from the fashionable French and Italian restau-
rants. The ocean is never more than a few blocks away. In the cloudless
blue sky, huge gulls are circling, filling the air with their throaty cries.

Nestled among trendy boutiques and lively cafes is a store called
Things from Heaven, referred to by locals as the *Angel Store*. In the
windows, statues of angels are surrounded by a carpet of pink flowers.
Inside, there is a shrine dedicated to the Virgin of Guadalupe. It is covered
with hundreds of slips of white paper, on which visitors from around the
world have written prayers either asking, or expressing thanks, for a
miracle. In the back of the store is a small art gallery displaying paintings

by world-famous angel artist, Andy Lakey. On a recent visit to the store, Andy was surrounded by a throng of people, all anxious to consult him.

* * * * *

Andy

A few years ago, I could never have envisaged that I would become an artist, and the new direction my life would take. I was a pretty successful car salesman, and was making good money — but everything I earned was spent on feeding my drug addiction.

One New Year's Eve in 1986, I hit the freebase pipe as usual, but this time something went terribly wrong. My heart began to beat as though it would burst out of my chest, and my skin felt as if it were on fire. I started to feel my whole body shutting down, and knew I was about to die. I crawled into the shower and managed to turn on the cold water. For the first time since I was eight years old, I prayed, begging God to spare me.

"I will never take drugs again," I promised, "and I will do something worthwhile with my life to help others."

As I spoke, I felt something swirling around me like a tornado. I couldn't see them in detail, but seven glowing beings of light were circling the lower part of my body, spiraling upward until they reached my heart. At this point, they merged into a single being, exactly like the figure I now depict in my paintings.

The being embraced me, and I felt a rush of unconditional love that seemed to transport me into another dimension. I saw a thousand planets with thousands of poles of light extending through them and into the void. Inside each pole were millions of tiny figures of light, and outside there were hundreds more, including me, all waiting to enter. I tried to get inside a pole, but I was bounced back from it, and then I woke up. I was in the emergency room, with an IV in each arm. I had survived an overdose.

I had made a promise to God, and I stopped taking drugs cold turkey.

For the next three years, I worked during the day, and instead of taking drugs each night when I came home, I started to draw pictures of what I'd experienced during my NDE. As time passed, I found myself becoming more and more frustrated. I knew there was something I was meant to do, but I didn't know what it was.

One morning, a beam of light shone through the wall, and touched me on the forehead. I felt a tingling sensation run through my entire body, and time seemed to stand still. Three angels stood before me. They didn't speak, but they relayed their message to me telepathically, and told me:

Andy you have been spared because you have a mission. You are going to create 2,000 angel paintings by the year 2000. We will take care of everything: we will teach you to paint, give you the specific art techniques you will use and create the necessary circumstances for your work to be a success.

They did exactly what they had promised, and things started to happen through a series of events I would formerly have termed *coincidences* or *accidents*. Within a few months, I had created enough angel paintings to hold an exhibition, which sold out. One buyer was a vacationing monsignor, who, upon his return to Rome, spread the news about my work. A few weeks later, I received a call from the Vatican; Pope John Paul 2 wished to buy a painting. I sent the Pontiff the first painting in my series.

Today, my work hangs in museums and art galleries all around the world, and the textured form of the paintings, that the angels guided me into, makes them visible to the blind. I didn't know it at the time, but God had another plan for my art, and I wasn't to find out what it was until a mysterious set of synchronistic events introduced me to Keith and Francesca Richardson, the owners of the angel store.

* * * * *

You can feel Francesca's Latin warmth and openness. She was born in Nicaragua, and raised in a devout Roman Catholic family. She firmly believed in God, angels, and miracles, and never dreamed a day would come when she would turn away from her faith. And yet, that is exactly what happened. In 1975, she met, Keith, and fell in love with him, but because he was divorced, she wasn't allowed to marry him in a Catholic church. The priests said their union would be a sin, and refused to sanction it. Their cold, uncaring attitude shocked her. She married Keith in spite of the Church's objection, and renounced her faith altogether. For the next eleven years, she lived with no God, no religion, and no angels in her home.

Keith used to pride himself on his logical mind. He believed there was a rational explanation for everything. God, religion, angels, and the afterlife were all just crutches for wishful thinkers who couldn't face reality as it was. Armed with impressive degrees in psychology and anthropology, he was quite an expert in the field, and researched Virgin Mary cults for many years. His findings only served to confirm his opinion of how amazingly gullible people could be. Later, he used his talents to work in market research, fundraising and public relations, and he was successful. He gave himself full credit for his achievements. If you'd told him that one day he would be forced to acknowledge that angels and a higher power had been at work in his life, he would have called you a fool.

* * * * *

Keith and Francesca

In 1986, an event occurred that rattled our complacent attitude, by a strange coincidence; it was also the year in which Andy had his near-death experience. We were on vacation and visiting the shrine of the Virgin of Guadalupe, in Mexico City.

The Virgin of Guadalupe is the patron saint of Mexico, and she is famous for performing thousands of healing miracles throughout the world. The Virgin first appeared in 1531 to Juan Diego, an Aztec Indian, who had converted to Christianity. He saw her on a hill outside Mexico City. She told him to tell the local bishop to build a church on the very spot where he was standing. He ran to the bishop's residence, and, after a long wait, was given an audience. Jaun Diego described his vision of the Virgin Mary and gave the bishop her message about erecting a church.

The bishop told Juan that he would need proof. Juan returned to the hilltop and again had a vision of the Virgin Mary. He told her of the bishop's skepticism, and she gave him a bunch of roses, which he placed in his *tilma* (cloak). He showed them to the bishop, who was impressed; it was the middle of winter, and roses never bloomed at that time of year. But what finally convinced him of the validity of the vision was something he saw as Juan opened his cloak — embossed therein was an image of the Virgin Mary, which was not only beautiful, but had been formed using some method that was totally unknown at the time. A miracle was declared.

In the late nineteenth century, the Roman Catholic Church set about exposing fraudulent miracles from the past, and the Virgin of Guadalupe was on their list. The *tilma* was given a scrupulous examination. When viewed through a microscope, the cloak revealed another wonder that had never been seen before, and one that was clearly a technical impossibility in the sixteenth century: inside the pupils of the Virgin's eyes, there was a reflection of Juan Diego. The Church immediately reconfirmed the validity of the miracle.

As we were preparing to leave for our vacation, a friend called, and asked, "Please can you visit the shrine, and light a candle for my sick mother?" We felt we couldn't refuse, and that's how we ended up at the shrine. During the visit, we used up a reel of film; we thought our friend would like to have some souvenirs of the trip. We took pictures of our sons buying the candle, putting it on the altar, lighting it, and so on. As an afterthought, we also got two shots of Juan Diego's *tilma*.

When we returned home and had the film developed, we made a puzzling discovery: in one of the two photos of the *tilma*, the cloak was facing the wrong way. Photography experts were baffled. The anomaly could not be due to a printing error, since a color print cannot be success-fully printed from a reversed negative. We then discussed the matter with several religious authorities, but they could give us no rational expla-nation either.

"It's your own private miracle," they told us, "and it's for you alone to discover its meaning."

Following this incident, our life soon began to take off, and my new fundraising job with the Episcopal Church enabled us to move to a beautiful ranch set on four acres. We began to feel a strong connection with the Episcopalian faith, and the whole family converted. We were sure we had found our calling. The "miracle" appeared to have worked magic in our lives.

However, after a few years, everything came crashing down. Administrative changes in the church meant that I lost my job, and the life that went with it. I tried to find another position, but with no success, and so we began to consider opening up our own business. I'd become experi-enced in setting up thrift stores in my fundraising work, so we decided to open one in downtown Ventura. We searched for a place for several months, but by this time our credit was destroyed, and no landlord wanted to rent to us. We had exhausted our savings, and were on the verge of becoming homeless.

Around this time, Francesca started to have recurring dreams. In every dream, she would look up into the sky, the clouds would part, and hundreds of angels would appear. They didn't speak; they just smiled at her, and she smiled back. Then one night, she had a different dream in which a childhood friend from Nicaragua, who had died the previous year, came to her.

"What are you doing here Alejandro?" she asked. "You're supposed to be dead."

"I've been sent to bring you this," he replied. He showed her a beautiful, gold-bound book.

"What kind of book is this? Francesca asked.

"Read it with me, and you'll find out," replied Alejandro.

In her dream, she read the entire book. It was all about angels. It said that they are Beings of Light; they are God's messengers and they bring God's love, peace and joy into the world. Francesca woke up from this profound experience determined that we would forget our plans for a thrift store, and instead open an angel store.

To begin with, I thought Francesca's dreams were pure fantasy, and that they were a result of the enormous stress and pressure we were under. However, she seemed so unwavering and resolute that I decided to check the idea out.

Later that day, we again walked down Main Street, looking for a space to rent. During the night a new sign had gone up. It was on a storefront in the worst part of town. In those days prior to Ventura's facelift that meant it was really bad. There was an abandoned liquor store and a twenty-four hour porno shop on one side and above us there was a hotel for transients.

Street people lived in the recessed entrance to the store. Inside, there were holes in the walls. The filthy carpet was hidden under a two-inch layer of cigarette butts, and old, rotting couches were strewn everywhere. Having just been fumigated, the place was full of dead rats and cockroaches.

It seemed an unthinkable location for an angel store, and yet we both had the feeling that this was where we were meant to be. We reached an agreement with the owner, who was glad that anyone was interested in renting the place. Our families thought we were insane, and we too, still had moments of terrible doubt. As a compromise, we decided to open a gourmet food store and sell a few angel knickknacks on the side, just to honor the dream.

We opened the store in April, 1995, and within a few months, we had taken all the food off the shelves. It had become clear that customers were only interested in the angels. We filled the store with angel gifts and artifacts, and set up a shrine to the Virgin of Guadalupe, which included the two photographs we'd taken in Mexico. Business boomed. Two months later, Monsignor O'Brian, from the nearby Buenaventura Mission, came to bless the store. He told us that our building was on sacred land that had once been the mission gardens.

One day, a lady came into the store and fell in love with the place. We had a conversation, and she said, "You must contact Andy Lakey and ask to exhibit his paintings. I used to work for him a few years ago, and I know his art is meant to be in your store." She was curiously insistent. We thought about the idea, but it seemed ridiculous. Why would a world-renowned artist with galleries all over the world, want to exhibit in our small struggling business?

We did contact Andy, though, and he astonished us by agreeing to our request. This is how Andy describes what happened:

I get hundreds of requests like this every year and usually turn them down. As I already had over a hundred galleries selling my work throughout the world, I had no intention of opening a new one. For some reason, however, I felt guided by God. Something made me think that this request from Keith was important. Some Divine force was urging me to call him back. I had received guidance like this before and knew that I had to follow God's directions.

Following the call from Andy, we started off with three small angel paintings, which were exhibited in the back of the store. Extraordinary events soon started to take place. When we ran our hands over the paintings, our palms became hot and we felt a tingling sensation similar to pins and needles. Without being forewarned in any way, customers started to report having a similar experience. This was disturbing enough, but then things got stranger...

One day, a Native American came into the store. We asked if we could help him with anything, and he replied, "My name is Sundance and I was happy in my life. I had a good job, a wife and two young sons, until one day a drunk driver hit our car head-on, and all members of my family were killed instantly. Since the accident, I've given up on life and lost everything. I think that God has abandoned me." We could sense that he was full of anger and grief and invited him to spend a little time in the art gallery, thinking that it might help him find some peace. He reluctantly agreed, and after finding a painting that he was drawn to, he put his hands over it and prayed for his wife and children. He stood still for several moments and then began to weep.

Then he turned to us and said:

I've been so wrong about everything. When I touched the paintings, it seemed like the heavens were opening up, and I saw my wife and children almost as clearly as I can see you now. They spoke to me. They told me they were happy where they were, and said I should stop worrying about them. Then I heard God speaking to me. He told me I was on the wrong path. He said I was needed back on the reservation, and that I would be working with orphaned children.

We were astounded, but since then hundreds of customers have made contact and seen deceased relatives and friends appear to them through the paintings. It's as if there is a portal in the back of our store, a doorway to the other side. When someone is grieving the loss of a loved one, this form of communication can have a miraculous effect. It brings renewed faith and hope, and it awakens a deeper appreciation for the invisible spiritual world that lies beyond our own. Sometimes, as in the case of Sundance, specific messages are given and can help transform a person's life.

We feel we have been given a job here to do, and we'll stay just as long as God, or the Higher Power that manifest in our lives, wants us to. It's not what we imagined ourselves to be doing, but it is the purpose that

God had in mind for us. His voice can be heard everywhere, and in every-thing that surrounds us, but we just needed to listen to his message. It seems that we needed to hit rock bottom — to lose our livelihood and all our possessions — before we were ready to hear what he wanted from us. But everything we lost in our former lives has now been regained a thousand times. Our work here is a blessing, and we have the privilege of being able to help others understand that physical death is a threshold that leads us into a new dimension of existence. There is no greater joy than that!

* * * * *

Andy remained busy for a long time, and the Gallery was crowded with people waiting to consult him. They would bring a photo of their deceased fiend or loved one, and he draws the impressions that come through to him.

He says:

I'm neither a prophet, nor a psychic, and I don't claim to know what the messages emanating from my art mean. But I believe that following my near-death experience in 1986, God gave me the ability to channel his love through my art. The messages that come through me are like a laser beam, as I paint them onto the canvas, and are very consistent. They always bring love, hope and a new understanding, and I have the feeling that this experience often directs people to finding a higher purpose in their lives.

A woman in the store, named Claudia, explains how she was able to come to terms with her son's death through touching one of Andy's paintings:

A friend brought me here a few months ago. I was in really bad shape. I had lost both my son and my father within a few months. I found a picture here in the gallery; it was one that had a dark silhouette with an angel in the middle. I shut my eyes and put my hands over it, and I started to experience a strange feeling. As I half-opened my eyes, I could see a shadow moving on the wall; it looked like angel wings flapping. Then I saw my dad; he was standing up and my son was sitting down in front of him. They were both smiling at me. The scene was very colorful and peaceful. I knew then that they were both okay. My son died young — his life hadn't been very happy and he'd gone through a lot of pain. I was so happy to see he was with my dad. He was reaching up towards the light, and I knew I had to let him go, and trust that he was in a better place.

* * * * *

Walking down by the ocean, following Andy's session at the store, the white foamy waves tumbled in and out, and a light breeze filled the air. The dying sunset became a bright red glow on the edge of the horizon. It gradually faded away, replaced by the light of the full new moon. In this setting, the majesty of nature provided yet another image of the capacity for renewal and rebirth, one that is also reflected in the messages from the reality of an afterlife that emanate through Andy and his angel paintings.

SUZANNE'S STORY

*I ought to be grieved at death, if I were not persuaded that I am going
to other Gods who are wise and good*
Socrates

*Dr. Suzanne De Wees began her spiritual practice of Yoga and meditation
in the 1970's. A decade later, she started to receive guidance from the
non-physical dimension, which became the foundation of her mediumistic
talents, and introduced the power of a Divine Presence into her life.*

The Southern Cassadaga Spiritualist camp is situated in Volusia County,
Florida, about twenty-five miles southwest of Daytona Beach. It was
founded in 1875, by a medium called George Colby. As a child, Colby
was told in a séance that one day that he would become involved in estab-
lishing a spiritualist community.

Later, this prediction came true: the young Colby traveled throughout
the Midwest, and was led to the wilderness of central Florida by an Indian
spirit guide called Seneca, a name which means "rocks beneath the
water." Colby was told by Seneca that he was to found a psychic center
where mediums, healers, and spiritualists could form a community. When
Colby arrived at his final destination, he was suffering from tuberculosis
but, according to legend, he was cured by the healing waters of a small
spring found on the land.

The Spiritualist community began to form in 1875. In 1895, Colby
filled out a homestead claim on the land, and gave over thirty-five acres
to the Cassadaga Spiritualist Camp Meeting Association. The small town
now consists of fifty-seven acres and fifty-five homes, and hasn't
changed very much since it was established at the turn of the last century.
It retains the charm of a village-like atmosphere that is reflected in its
narrow streets and picturesque buildings, many of which are flavored
with a colonial architectural style.

The surrounding countryside is beautiful, and provides a peaceful haven for many forms of wildlife; it is famous for the white swans that are seen to gather on the many little lakes and ponds that form part of the local scenery.

The land is said to be situated over an energy vortex or ley line, which enables etheric vibrations and communication with the spirit world to take place. Today, visitors flock to Cassadaga in their thousands to consult with the many mediums and spiritual healers who make this serene area their permanent home.

* * * * *

Suzanne

My spiritual journey began when I started to practice the ancient eastern traditions of Yoga and meditation in the 1970's. I became a founding member of the Kripalu Center for Yoga and Health, and lived in the ashram that was established by Yogi Amrit Desai. I also studied with meditation masters from Burma, India and Nepal and, over the years, participated in ongoing retreats in the Vipassana and Dzogchen traditions.

A decade later, the altered state of consciousness that I entered during my meditation enabled me to get in touch with my ability to channel spirit. This form of awareness expanded far beyond the day-to-day world, and was not limited by the constraints of linear distance and time. Physicists refer to it as the "non-local" mind, and this fascinating phenomenon serves to connect us to each other, and to the world at large. It also allows us to describe, experience, and influence activities occurring anywhere in space and time. I believe that it was the purification from the years of Yoga that allowed this quantum sense of inter-connectedness to filter through me.

One day, after completing my practice, I went to my computer and found myself beginning to type in questions — and I started to receive replies. This form of communication with the spirit world is known as automatic writing. It's something that anyone can practice to open themselves up to receiving messages from other realms of existence. But, to begin with, the answers were difficult to understand, because they came through in a form of old English that was not familiar to me. I had to look up certain words and spellings to make sense of what the spirit was communicating to me.

This period of automatic writing opened the door to my ability to act as a medium and get in touch with non-physical dimensions. During this time, I contacted a guide called Blessian and started to work with him, as I began to do readings for people. He later introduced me to an entity known as Monseria, who described herself as a star teacher rather than a guide, and welcomed me to the *community of spirit*, saying:

I introduce myself to you as Monseria. I bring the light of the galaxies to you in this simple text. Among these words, you may find intrigue in the possibility of renewed health, well-being and happiness. I have brought you teachings from the stars for eons, and bring simpler guidance to you at this time. I am not of a physical body; I am a body of Light.

My guidance is towards quieting the mind, deepening the breath and opening to the Light. Since all wisdom is contained in the soul, there is no further wisdom I can offer. I can provide a context in which you slow down to attune to that which is true and that which is known.

There is a great deal of reason in your lives to rush along, to make plans and to project into the future. My gift is to bring that reasoning to a dead halt, and to acknowledge the infinite capacity which you have to relax and to attain peace.

My role is in telling the soul the truth: each individual is capable of living in a much brighter landscape. My encouragement is for everyone to be brighter, but not better. May each person take the time needed to experience the light of their lives through spiritual practices.

As I started to use my abilities as a medium, I continued with my Yoga, and practiced under the tutelage of a great Kundalini Yoga Master, Swami Kri Palu, for my first four years. In 1994, I attended a month-long meditation retreat. During the deep meditation, I was given the table of contents to a book that Monseria requested to channel through me. So, I took a sabbatical from the Kripalu Center with my husband, and went to Key Largo. As I didn't want the workings of my conscious mind to interfere with Monseria's teachings, I worked backwards and completed the manuscript, which served to further extend my knowledge, and gave me direct access to a wider world of consciousness.

After twenty years, my husband and I left the ashram and moved to Florida. While studying at a massage school to get a Florida massage therapy license, I started to attend spiritual healing classes at the Southern Cassadaga Spiritualist Camp, which was situated nearby.

During this period, my mother had become seriously ill, and I thought, "I really don't know very much about the end of life." This insight led me to start volunteering in a hospice three days a week, and I interned as a chaplain while completing my Ph.D., in Integral Health. As I started this work, I realized that a deep, profound acquaintance with death and the dying process was the only true way for me to learn more about life

Even though I had been active as a medium and spiritual healer for fifteen years, I had to undergo the rigorous training carried out at Cassadaga, in order to gain my certification to have a private practice within the community. This included providing lectures, leading meditations, and delivering spirit messages in front of up to sixty people and medium elders twice a week. Up until this time, I had made contact with spirit guides, but now, through my training, I began to contact the spirits of deceased relatives and friends.

In 1995, my mother died at her home a few days before Christmas, and there was a festive Christmas tree in her living room. The day after she made her transition, a white dove that had been decorating the tree was found in the middle of the floor, along with a second ornament that I had given her years before. There was no gust of air blowing through the room, and no way the ornaments could have just simply fallen that far from the tree; I sensed she was communicating with me and letting me know that she was all right. Often, a spirit will manifest in this way to bring comfort and assurance to those still living.

We eventually bought a home in Cassadaga, and I became a certified healer and medium at the camp. I found that I shared the Spiritualist philosophy, which acknowledges that loved ones and friends may choose to communicate after death. Spiritualism is not based on the teachings of any particular spiritual masters, but values evidential information gained from spirit entities, and people who come to the Southern Cassadaga Spiritualist Camp to consult the practitioners have good and positive experiences.

I find that when people come to consult me, only about thirty percent of them are really interested in contacting a deceased relative. It is mainly parents who have lost a child who want to make contact with the spirit of their loved one, because the grief is so intense at the loss. The rest are seeking guidance from a higher power, in order to help them find their own divinity and true essence.

Often, a deceased relative will communicate a message to me before the client makes an appointment to consult me, and sometimes they will make themselves known by some kind of psychical activity. One day, I was visiting a lady and she was talking about her deceased son, when suddenly, a picture of him fell off a bookcase and made his spirit presence known to us. Often the presence of a loved one's spirit is felt more keenly in people's homes, shortly after they have made their transition.

My belief as a medium and spiritual healer is that our intention is the same as our life force, and that prayer or meditation can direct that life force or intention to connect with our natural essence (the God Consciousness) in the present moment. When we pray or meditate, we are directing our life force to the present moment, and that is when we receive guidance from Spirit.

Cassadaga is a powerful place, and its foundations rest on over a hundred years of Spiritualism. People feel the difference in energy when they arrive here. Interest in the Spiritual church waned in the middle of this century, but has now revived, and we often have full attendance at our Sunday services.

Today, growing numbers of people are attracted to the philosophy of the Spiritualist church, because they have discovered that earthly existence is not about accruing a string of degrees, or gaining material success; it is about finding the meaning in life itself. The scientific and philosophical beliefs of Spiritualism serve only to help in this quest, and seek to heal mankind.

* * * * *

In 1992, when Suzanne was in India, she was fortunate enough to meet Mother Teresa who, in her service to humanity, founded her own order to minister to all those who felt rejected by society and converted an abandoned Hindu Temple into the Kalighat Home for the Dying, which offers free hospice care for the poor. Mother Teresa believed in ecumenism that embraces one God in all his many manifestations. As she took Suzanne's hands, something very profound passed between them. They stood chatting for a moment and, as Suzanne looked at her, she witnessed the Christ consciousness — the presence of divine love — reflected in her eyes. Spiritualism and mediumship provide a way of connecting us all through spirit, to this same universal life source and presence of divine love.

CAROL'S STORY

Should we not offer up a prayer first of all to the local deities?
Socrates

Prayer is a way of communicating with a higher power, and ancient texts verify that the existence of prayer dates back many thousands of years. All the world's major religions have various forms of this devotional act. Prayer acts as a dialogue between the Divine realms and earthly existence. The power of prayer can bring about transformation and healing.

At the end of her lectures, Carolyn Myss used to tell a story about a woman who had a near-death experience following a horrific car crash. As the badly-injured woman left her body, she could hear the thoughts of all of the people who were stuck in a traffic jam that resulted from her auto accident. At one point, she noticed some twinkling "lights" coming towards her. They entered her body, and she felt nourished and loved. She wondered where the lights had come from. Suddenly, she was transported to the fifth car that was caught up in the jam. She saw and heard the driver, who was inside the vehicle, praying for whoever was in the accident. Before returning to her body, she got the license plate of the car. Following her recovery, she managed to track down this person's address, and personally delivered a dozen red roses. She explained that she was the person the driver had been praying for.

* * * * *

Carol

On my wedding day, which should have been the happiest day of my life, three of my friends came up to me and said, "Do you know who your mother-in-law reminds us of? They went on to ask me if I had ever seen the film *101 Dalmations*, and remembered the character of Cruella de Ville!

Sadly, this unfortunate caricature very accurately depicted my husband's mother, Jean, in appearance, tone, and actions. She picked and started a fight when my husband and I returned from our honeymoon, and the constant friction and rows soon doomed our marriage. The divorce negotiations ended up taking twice as long as our marriage had survived; Jean paid for my husband's attorney, and they were hell-bent on suing me for alimony. During this difficult and painful period, I took solace in my charity work, which had trained me as a volunteer in hospice, to ensure that no one need die alone.

One day, sometime later, while I was at work, I found out that Jean was on hospice care; the doctors did not expect her to live for more than a few days, and my ex-husband, Alan, had no support in caring for her. As soon as I heard this news, I closed the door to my office and prayed in silence that God would surround her with love and light, and make her transition an easy one. Later that day, I called and left Alan a message, saying that if he would like me to sit with Jean for a night so that he could get some sleep, I would be happy to do so.

I didn't hear anything back, so I went to my regular spiritually-orien-tated study group meeting. I added Jean's name to the list of people in transition from this world that we wanted to pray for. At the end of our group meditation, in addition to having her name read out loud, there was a special moment of silence when my colleagues were praying to amplify whatever prayer I was offering. I prayed once more for Jean to be surrounded with love and light, and that God would make her transition a peaceful one.

After the meeting ended, I checked again for messages from my ex-husband. There were none, so I went home. I felt quite exhausted, and crawled into bed and turned out the light. Within moments, I felt as if someone were in the room. I switched the light back on, and discovered that directly in front of me was a pearlescent figure. It was solid in appearance, because I couldn't see the wall behind it. I was startled by this manifestation, and screamed. Immediately, the figure collapsed, as if withdrawing from the veil it had pushed through to visit me. I never took my eyes off it until long after the silhouette of its shadow had started to fade, and once again, I was looking through where it had been and could see the wall across the room. I knew this apparition had been Jean.

Oddly, my first thought was, "Well, I'm glad that doesn't happen to me very often!" I thought I would call a mutual friend of mine and my ex-husband's, to see if Jean had made her transition. So when I woke up in the morning, it was the first call I made. The friend confirmed that Jean had indeed passed the night before. I then enquired as to the exact time of death, and discovered it was during the period that we had been praying for her.

It's a strange and fascinating thought that the person with whom I had by far the most difficult relationship in my life ended up giving me the greatest gift that I had ever received. For I knew this was confirmation that we do survive the death of the physical body. It also provided me with the knowledge that I had grown enough to be able to feel compassion, and sincerely pray for someone who had caused me such a lot of grief.

Later, I was to discover that Jean had also changed a lot during the final stages of her life. She had come to realize that many of the ideas and concepts that she had spent a lifetime valuing were irrelevant, and that loving her children was the only thing that really mattered.

* * * * *

Carol discovered the amazing healing power of prayer when her former mother-in-law was in the dying process. She had always believed that each of us has a soul that survives physical death, but her experience with Jean was the first time that she had ever received such concrete evidence. For this profound insight, she will always be grateful.

SANDRA'S STORY

...our recent argument and others as well compel us to believe that the
soul is immortal
Socrates

Sandra Cook started to receive messages from the spirit world at an early
age. Both her grandmother and great grandmother were mediums, and
fostered her ability to communicate with other realms of consciousness.
Sandra uses her gift in her work, as a spiritual counselor and medium.
She is also a full-time minister in the Spiritualist church.

The drive from Ojai, to Santa Barbara, is beautiful on this late spring day.
Highway 150 meanders along the back route as it winds through the
mountains where nature comes alive in its entire splendor, revealing a
landscape that is verdant and lush. Nestled in a valley is Lake Casitas,
which fills following the late rains, acting as a wildlife sanctuary for
many birds and animals. New foliage and blossom on the trees create cool
arbors along the country roads, from which the sun peeks through the
gently rustling branches.

The Spiritualist Church of the Comforter is located on Garden Street,
in the heart of the town. It has an active, growing community. Sandra, the
full time minister, took some time to talk before preparing for a
Wednesday evening Message Service and described how she evolved her
spiritual ability to become a full-time medium.

* * * * *

Sandra

As we grow up, we are taught to trust and develop our five senses, and
our sixth sense is ignored or discounted. As a result, it atrophies.
Nevertheless, we are all aware to some extent of our intuition operating.

It's the little voice that warns us of danger, or makes us think of someone when they are about to call. It is our link to the spiritual world, and yet it is often perceived as a strange, alarming kind of magic, or a crazy hunch. However, when we welcome this intuitive faculty into our world, we see that it is simply the spontaneous operation of our deeper nature, or soul, which we surely wish to encourage rather than subdue. When we are open to intuitive impressions, we are allowing ourselves to be guided by a wise part of our nature which sees much farther than our five senses and our rational mind. This part of us is wonderfully creative, and it never fails to improve and enrich our lives.

My great grandmother was psychic, and so was my grandmother, so I just grew up thinking that it was perfectly natural. I started receiving messages when I was very young. If this ability is not shut down; it just stays with you and, like your other senses, continues to develop. When I look back to my childhood, I remember it being one that closely resembled the childhood of the character Harry Potter, as described in the J. K. Rowling books. Although my mother was not open to psychic phenomena at that time, I spent a lot of time at my grandmother's house, which was just down the street. It was a fine education in mediumship, a sort of "Hogwart," for we experienced paranormal phenomena all the time, and I thought nothing of it.

I was thirty-three years old before I thought there was anything unusual about my ability. One day, a woman asked me, "Can you teach me to do what you do?" I was surprised, and answered, "But I thought everyone had this ability." She answered, "No, they don't," and I guess this was the first time I realized that my gift might be a little unusual.

When I was young, my family attended an Anglican church but, as I grew older, I started to go to services at a Spiritualist church. We used to attend the message service, and the minister would go up and down the rows in the congregation, giving out messages. But she never had one for me. On one occasion, I asked her, "Why does nothing ever come through for me?" She looked at me, and answered, "Because you already have all the answers. You're doing what you are supposed to be doing, so you aren't getting any messages.

I got used to communicating with the spirit world and seeing dead spirits, so when my great grandmother died and everyone was crying at the service, I turned round and said, "Why are you crying? She's standing just over there." My mother was upset and told me to be quiet but, from an early age, I knew that physical death wasn't the end, and so didn't understand what all the fuss was about!

When I was about seven years old, I gave a strong message to a friend of my mother's who had come to visit. She was due to catch a flight home, and I knew that the plane would have trouble clearing the mountains. I told her not to go, and again, my mother was furious. But this premonition proved to be right, because that flight later crashed into the mountaintops. My grandmother always encouraged me to trust the messages and images that spontaneously came into my mind, and I learned to have confidence in the process.

When I got married, my husband had not been raised in a similar way, although he gradually became open in this respect, and started to expand his own awareness. He was rather spooked at the beginning though, because we had only been married for a year and a half when, one night, I kept waking up. A lot of people don't realize that as well as communicating with spirits, mediums also often help with taking people over to the other side. Normally, guides will come to escort the dying person but, if there is a huge-scale disaster, we will assist in this work. It so happened that there had been a terrible accident in India, and two trains full of people had crashed into the side of a mountain. All that night, I had been traveling to the other side to help get these people across.

When I woke up in the morning, I told my husband what had happened. He went straight out and got a newspaper. When he returned, he was shocked, and I said, "What's wrong?" He replied, "Nothing," and then laid the paper down in front of me. The open page showed photos and a description of the crash. At that moment, my husband realized the full implications of my work, and it surprised him. However, he is now training to become a medium, although he really had to work hard to open up this ability because, in his family, spiritual beliefs were all about hell, fire, and brimstone. This narrow way of thinking closes all the chakras down, and they have to be gradually reactivated.

Early on in my marriage, I became very ill with cancer. By the time it was diagnosed, I was only given a short time to live. The illness started my work with healing, as I began to visualize myself well. I did this visualization every hour, and although it was a·fifteen-year battle to finally overcome the illness, the day finally came when the tests reported me to be cancer free. It was during this period that we moved to Phoenix, Arizona. My husband was offered job opportunities in different areas of the country, and we chose Phoenix because of its warmer climate, which would benefit my health.

Serious illness really helps you to value the things in life that are important. From an early age, I knew that I was to become a minister, and I think this experience was given to me so that I could understand and empathize with others in a similar situation. When you are faced with losing your life — that's the moment you really start to appreciate the beauty of the moment, and the importance of making the most of our short time on planet earth. My own experience developed and expanded my ability to become a medical intuitive, and to become involved in healing work.

In Phoenix, I found a Spiritualist church to attend, and started to complete the formal training to become a certified medium. I studied the Morris Pratt method of mediumship, which is well-recognized in the Spiritualist world. The founder of the institute, Morris Pratt, was very interested in psychic phenomena and Spiritualism. He saw that there was a need for educated mediums to be able to instruct people about the religion. Pratt was supposedly told, by his Red Indian guide, of a place where there were richly-yielding metal deposits. With this information, he started a company known as The Ashland Mine of Ironwood, in

Michigan. He declared that if he became rich, he would donate part of his money to Spiritualism. Within a few months, the prophecy from his guide came true. He kept his word, and with his newfound wealth he opened a temple in 1859, dedicated to the teachings of Spiritualism. The building encompassed a chapel, lecture rooms, office and dormitory. It soon got the reputation of being the "spook's temple," but eventually gained acclaim across the land. The temple, known as "Whitewater," was recognized as being the center of modern Spiritualism.

I started training, and began to meditate with my spirit teachers and guides. Although I had always done this from an early age, the practice became more formal as I sat in circle with the class and got feedback on the messages coming through.

When I was near the end my training and had become a licensed minister, I started looking for a church to work from. There were two vacancies, and one was in Santa Barbara. The church here had been looking for someone for two years. They liked the way I presented my lectures and classes, and offered me the job. The original church had been a focal point for the newly-founded Spiritualist organization located in Summerland, which was laughingly referred to as "Spooksville." Despite the jokes, the camp started to grow and as many as two or three hundred people would regularly attend meetings. As Spiritualism developed, so did Summerland, with its oil and natural gas resources. In 1951, a freeway was constructed through the town, and the church had to find a new home. The church board found a small building that had been a former Jewish synagogue, here in Garden Street.

The work I do is not the same as that of John Edward, or James Van Praagh, as seen on their TV shows. It's a whole different ball game, because I work with people grieving over a lost child, or people experiencing a death in the family where there has been no resolution. My job is very hard to deal with on a day-to-day basis. It's not about ego, or fame and fortune; it's about helping people, and it's a calling to be of service to others. I have to explain to heartbroken parents that sometimes children don't always come to stay, because they may have finished what they needed to accomplish here, in a very short time. The main focus of my work is to help people understand that there is no death; there is only a physical change in which we drop the body, but the essence of our being continues to exist in another form. I try to encourage people to live fully in the present moment, and appreciate the beauty of life.

The messages I give people contain information that is pertinent to their lives; some take it and some ignore it. Often, people come in with a list of questions they want answers to, and usually they are about relationships, jobs, or the future. I can't predict the way Spirit will answer, and sometimes they totally ignore the questions asked because they have important information to give the person.

A short while ago, a young man came to one of the message services. Spirit came through, and I was directed to ask the man, "Are you completing your dissertation?" He replied that he was, but added that he was not interested in discussing this subject, because he had more important questions that he wanted answers to. However, Spirit was emphatic, and a message came through that specifically advised him to check his work, because he had left something really important out. The young man left; he was disappointed and upset. However, a week later he called. He told me that he had recently discovered that an important section was missing from his work. That's the way Spirit can come through — the messages received are not consciously what the individual wants to hear, but contain information about what they need to hear.

I am often asked about what happens to our animal friends, when they make their transition. The answer is that all animals go to the spirit world, where they are taken care of and wait for their loved ones, or join them if they have already departed from earthly life. They communicate to help people through their grief and, sometimes, they leave this world in order to welcome their loved ones into the afterlife.

One day, I was doing a reading for a couple and I had a cockatoo make its presence felt. Neither of them had ever had such a bird, but they had friends who raised them, and each of these people had a particular bird they were close to. The cockatoo would not leave so, when the couple arrived back home after the reading, they called their friends and found them to be very upset. The husband's bird had died very abruptly. It had not been ill, or shown any sign of something being wrong, and the couple were very relieved to learn that the cockatoo was fine on Spirit side. The following week, the couple made a further call to their friends to see how they were doing, and the wife told them that her husband had died from a massive heart attack the day before. This was a case where the bird left first, in order to welcome his owner upon his arrival. The husband came through with the bird on numerous occasions, to help his wife cope with the grief caused by his transition.

I often have people come to consult me right after a pet leaves, and I can assure them that their animal has had a safe passage and is happy and well. One lady came very distraught after her very elderly cat died. The woman was not eating, and was very upset. Then I told her, "Fluff comes to see you a lot, especially in the evenings, and walks around the edge of the bed three times before finally lying down on the pillow next to you." The lady was shocked, but then said that she had felt Fluff's presence around her, and had noticed an indentation in her pillow that was in the shape of her cat. Once I could validate that Fluff was fine and still around, the woman perked up and started to take an interest in life again.

Dogs also come back to bring comfort, and to check in on their earthly family. They often appear to help and guide us through difficult times. For some people, they are easier to "see" or "feel" when they show up. On numerous occasions, a dog will show up to help with a new puppy or dog that has been brought into their owner's lives. Animals are very close to us, and bring a wonderful energy when they come to visit. People also bring their pets to me if there appears to be something wrong, and it's possible to psychically connect with them and discover the reason. Sometimes, this can be due to an illness or some form of anxiety.

Another aspect of my work is helping people make their transition to the other side. Sometimes, someone will die, but get trapped between this world and the next. I recall the case of a young Catholic man who had committed suicide. Because he had been brought up to believe that taking your own life was a sin, and that there was no salvation, he was trying to cling on to his life here, by staying near his wife and family. I needed to contact his dead grandmother in Spirit, and ask her to come and fetch him. She agreed, and came to take him over.

When individuals make their transition, they often try to communicate from the other side, just to let us know that they are all right. For example, people may smell their loved one's perfume in certain parts of the house. Sometimes, if the deceased was a pipe or cigarette smoker, relatives might detect the faint whiff of smoke, even though they cannot understand where this is coming from. The truth is that spirits communicate in these subtle ways to try and get our attention, but many people fail to notice. I tell people to stop and think if they notice such happenings, because it can greatly alleviate the grieving process to know that a loved one is still around, even though not physically present. On occasions, the presence of Spirit can be felt through strange noises or rappings on the wall; this also is nothing to be alarmed about. These kinds of manifestations often occur on the birthday of the deceased, or on some special occasion, like an anniversary of some kind.

Many people see a glimpse of other realms during an NDE. My daughter had this type of experience following a horse riding accident when she was thirteen. She was told that she could stay, but she knew how unhappy we would be without her, and decided to come back. She is now in training to become a medium herself. My daughter did have a twin sister, who did not reach full term and, in Spirit, she is my control for my trance work and decides who can come through and who can't. My husband acts as my control on this side. I go into a deep trance when it's important to provide the most direct channel for spirits to communicate through and, in this state, I certainly can't be in control myself. We have to learn how to communicate with Spirit, just as those in this realm of consciousness, have to learn to communicate with us.

I am often asked, "What's it like over on the other side?" The answer is that Spirit can manifest any environment through positive thoughts. Individuals who make their transition with a positive attitude adjust more quickly than those who leave in a negative state of mind. When we cross over, there is a life-review. It's a very lovely experience, in which there is no judgment; we just look back and see what we have accomplished in our lives. As on the earthly plane, there are stages of development and growth that take place in the Spirit world, when the essence or soul of the person has adjusted to their new surroundings.

As children, we are still very near the spiritual dimensions and often interact with our Spirit guides or ancestors. Many people think that interactions with imaginary friends are, in fact, a form of spiritual experience. It's such a shame that this early ability often disappears throughout the rest of a person's lifetime, and is only reactivated when the person is close to death.

As people engage with the dying process, they start to separate and detach from everyday life, and begin to dip in and out of this world and the hereafter; they can also start to communicate with Spirit. Often, we think these types of occurrences are merely delusions and they are dismissed, because the dying person may be suffering from dementia or Alzheimer's disease. But, if you listen carefully, you can hear accounts of conversations and visitations from entities who appear to assist and guide the dying person in their transition.

Some time ago my daughter, who has always enhanced her psychic ability, was looking after an old lady. No one else would spend the night with her, because her home was said to be full of spirits and the lady concerned was going back and forth between worlds. She had been married twice and both of her departed husbands, who disliked each other, were fighting in an upstairs room. All the commotion was keeping the old lady awake and fretful. In the end, my daughter got so fed up that she opened the door and shouted at the spirits, insisting that they all leave.

Suddenly, silence reigned once more, and she finally settled the lady down.

My mother, who is now in her eighties, has also finally come to terms with her heritage, and is now actively interested in Spiritualism. It took her some time, but she is now firmly convinced in the validity of my work. My grandson Andrew, who only survived here for sixty-one days, often makes his presence felt in the church. We will hear a tapping on the wall, and I know he's with us. So, it's really a family affair, on both sides of life.

The main point I would like to stress to people is that mediumship has a long history, which dates back to the early shamans or medicine doctors. There are recorded instances in all the sacred texts, and many of the secular writings, of otherworldly journeys. The ancient Egyptians and Greeks both had their seers, who were able to speak with the Gods, and there are many instances of spirit communication listed throughout the Christian Bible.

It was on March 31, 1848, which happened to be an Easter Sunday, that the advent of modern American Spiritualism took place through the now famous Fox sisters. Today there are churches and camps all the way across America and Europe.

Spiritual healing is also recognized in many sacred texts in both ancient and modern religions. A healer has the ability to channel healing energy from a higher source, and can help bring about cures for both mental and physical conditions. The primary manner of conducting this type of healing is through the laying-on of hands. Absent healing can also bring about positive results.

Psychic abilities are far more widespread than people think. Around 9/11, many ordinary individuals, not just psychics and psychic mediums, received information about the terrible tragedy that was to take place. People reported having dreams and visions that included towers, aircraft, and widespread destruction, but none of us were able to put the whole thing together. This was another instance where mediums were able to actively engage in rescue work, for many of these victims didn't even know that they had died, and needed help to transition over to the other side.

I enjoy my work enormously, and even though it can be tough at times, it's very rewarding to see the congregation continuing to grow, with more and more young people becoming interested and involved in the church. I to encourage them to make the most of their gifts and to work with their intuition, because becoming aware of our purpose in life can really help change attitudes and behavior. The most important thing about this work is that it's all about love and all done out of love; it's about improving our life here, and our future life on the other side.

* * * * *

At 6:15 p.m., several people start to trickle into the church. Sandra's husband greets them, and hands them message cards to write down their questions. The church feels cool with a very peaceful presence. Sandra slips into a trance, as she starts to do her first reading of the evening. Her communications and messages from the spirit world bring comfort and help to those seeking a sense of direction in their lives. For people in the grieving process, Sandra helps them come to the realization that their loved ones still exist in another form of consciousness.

JOHN AND MARY-ELLEN'S STORY

Rhythm and harmony find their way into the inward places of the soul
Plato

When John and Mary-Ellen's son, Roscoe, died suddenly from an undetected heart problem, the couple plunged into deep despair and depression. A bereavement counselor suggested they contact a psychic medium at the Spiritualist Church in Santa Barbara. They decided to give this a try, and were to find great comfort in communications from Roscoe's spirit, which confirmed that he was still very much alive in the afterlife.

It's a surprisingly cool day in Ojai. John and Mary-Ellen have come to escape the famous "June gloom" which settles along the neighboring coastline, but the sun remains hidden by swirling grey clouds. We are sitting in a Mexican restaurant that overlooks the park, where volunteers are busily clearing up the debris from the annual music festival that took place over the weekend. Three years have passed since Roscoe died. Although they still miss their son a great deal, John and Mary-Ellen tell us of their meeting with Sandra Cook at the Spiritualist Church of the Comforter, and how it helped to literally "save their lives."

* * * * *

John and Mary-Ellen

When our son, Roscoe, suddenly died from an undetected heart problem, Mary-Ellen and I went into a deep, crippling depression. We had always been so close and entwined in each other's lives. I'm a charter boat captain, and Roscoe grew up on the boat. Right from the start, he loved the life, and we always remember him as a small baby, crawling up from the stern in the mornings to wake us up and have a cuddle. Living in such a small space made us all very connected to each other, and we spent his early years cruising to many different places, including Panama and Mexico. We had a great life together; by the time Roscoe was twenty-five, he was a fully-licensed captain with his own boat moored in the same harbor. And every night, we always used to "sign-off" with each other, via our short-wave radios.

Roscoe appeared to be athletic, tanned, and very fit but, throughout his short life, he had suffered from debilitating bouts of asthma and eczema. Sadly, we didn't know that the drugs he was taking to combat his asthma attacks were also having adverse side effects on his heart. Sometimes, he complained of feeling his heart thumping so loudly in his chest that he worried about having a heart attack. We felt really badly after he'd died, because when he made these comments, we'd laugh them off, and say, "Oh Roscoe, don't be so dramatic." We never imagined that his heart had swollen to twice its normal size; he was such a young man and had seemed so full of life and future plans.

But gradually, Roscoe started to become depressed; he didn't feel good and seemed to lose his zest for life. Every morning, at 10:00 a.m., he would call and check to see what was happening work-wise, however, one day — he just didn't call. This was very unlike him, but we thought, "He must just be busy." The next day, he didn't call either and we had a terrible feeling that something was wrong. I decided to go over to his boat and make sure everything was all right, and found him lying dead in his bed. It was the most terrible shock, and we were both devastated. We'd only recently made plans for a trip together to Hawaii.

In our grief, we thought back to the time when the three of us had been on our previous boat, and were capsized by a hurricane. We were at sea for quite a long time, marooned in an inflatable raft, and had used all our flares. We were getting desperate, but Roscoe managed to get a signal going, and we were eventually picked up by a Korean freighter. We wouldn't have made it without him, and we wondered, "Why did we all manage to survive this life-threatening ordeal, only to have Roscoe snatched away from us at such an early age?" It seemed to make no sense.

Shortly after Roscoe's death, Mary-Ellen had an out-of-body experience; one night, she woke up to find herself looking down at her own body lying on the bed, and found herself moving towards the cockpit, where she saw Roscoe sitting. She asked him, "Roscoe, what are you doing here? You're supposed to be dead." He held up his hands, and said, "Look mum, no rash." He'd always had bad outbreaks of eczema around his wrists, and was showing her that they had now cleared up. Even though this experience gave us some comfort, we still found ourselves sinking deeper and deeper into depression. We'd always done things together, and now life didn't seem to have any meaning; we were both heartbroken as we started to deal with selling Roscoe's beloved boat and sorting through his affairs.

We did go for some bereavement counseling, but it didn't seem to help. One day, the counselor suggested that we visit a psychic medium at a Spiritualist church in Santa Barbara, who they believed, could put us in touch with Roscoe. We weren't connected to any particular church, so we decided to give this a try. Oddly enough, Roscoe had been very interested in Spiritualism, and had read many books on the subject shortly before he died. Looking back, we realize that Roscoe must have had a premonition, and knew that he was going to die young. Perhaps, he was already thinking and planning a way to continue communicating with us from the Spirit world.

The medium we were recommended to, Sandra Cook, is the head minister of the Spiritualist Church of the Comforter, in Santa Barbara, and there are also other trained mediums in the congregation. One of them is her husband, Paul, and when we first visited the church, he turned round, and exclaimed, "Oh my goodness, you've got metal in your body, in two different places!"

I was astounded, because this is absolutely true; I have a steel plate in my neck, and also metal in my shoulder. I thought to myself, "How in the world does he know that?" Then I realized: it wasn't from this world that he was getting his information!

We then had a reading from Sandra, who knew nothing about us; it was completely accurate, and so specific that it couldn't be put down to a few intuitive guesses or lucky hunches. Sandra told us that Roscoe was happy, and that he was working in the Spirit realm, with younger people. This made sense, because he had given up a promising football career in high school to become a student counselor. He'd been good at it too, and it seemed like he was carrying on with the job over there.

Ever since Roscoe's death, we'd been experiencing strange things taking place on the boat. Whenever we mentioned Roscoe's name, the television would just switch itself on. First of all, we thought that there was something wrong with the set, but the same thing kept occurring. After a while, we started to notice that the set had started to turn itself on at any time the day or night. Eventually, we got fed up and bought a new TV, but the same thing happened, and now we've got quite used to it. Sometimes, late at night, I'd be scared to death with a blanket over my head but, at the same time, I'd be staring at the screen, in case Roscoe came through. Occasionally, I think that I've detected a slight fuzzy shadow, but then it just disappears.

Then the phone started ringing and messages would be left; the voice sounded like Roscoe's, saying, "Okay, you guys should be able to hear me now." In the background, we could hear a sound like water running from a stream. We've also felt a cool current of air blowing through the boat, which results in small objects moving, or the curtains fluttering or, sometimes, the dishes sliding over the draining board. Sandra has reassured us that it's Roscoe, who is trying to let us know that he's still around.

During a reading a short while ago, Sandra told us that Roscoe was concerned about some damage to our boat. We checked everything, but couldn't find anything wrong. The messages persisted, so we eventually hauled the boat out of the water and discovered a small hole that could have ended up sinking the boat. This just seemed to confirm what Sandra had been telling us in the readings, when she said, "He loves you, and he's taking care of you."

The sessions we've had at the Spiritualist church have provided us with much-needed healing and hope and we feel that we're surrounded by a loving, supportive family. The church saved our lives, and gives us the sense that physical death is just the beginning of another level of existence. Mary-Ellen is sure that she's felt Roscoe's presence sitting next to her in one of the pews, and I've seen his form standing in the church. It's not just over when somebody dies. Of course, we miss physical contact with our son, and we would like to know exactly where he is. However, we do know that Roscoe is still with us; even though it may be in another form. And we know that he is influencing events from another place

Roscoe's death has made us much more aware, and we've come to realize that communication from the spirit world is much more common than we had previously thought. When Mary-Ellen went back to Rhode Island, to visit her family, she visited some very conservative friends; they asked her if she had any dreams or experiences of Roscoe since he died. She recounted her out-of-body experience and then, much to her astonishment, these people began to recount their own, similar experiences. But they would not have volunteered the information if Mary-Ellen had not been so open about describing what had happened to her.

After a hurricane destroyed our last boat, we had to start over; I was worried about managing all the heavy work, like the rigging, without Roscoe's help, but a lot of the supportive messages we received from him encouraged us to start living our lives again His messages give us the strength to carry on, and I've found myself suspended sixty feet above the ground on a winch, getting the boat ready for a trip we're planning to Hawaii. Our two daughters have given us wonderful grandchildren, and a couple of them are planning on coming with us. Gradually, our lives are beginning to have meaning again.

Our interactions with the Spiritualist church gave us faith and hope, and added a new spiritual dimension to our lives. Besides our regular meetings at the church, we have also joined an Anglican Bible study group, which we really enjoy. To begin with, we were too depressed to join in, but now we are fully involved, and it makes us feel a whole lot better.

* * * * *

Following their experiences with Sandra Cook, John and Mary-Ellen find it strange that the teachings of the Spiritualist church are regarded by some people as having to do with the occult. In reality, Spiritualism preaches the same message as all the other forms of religion and views the life of the soul or essence as being eternal, acknowledging an infinite intelligence that many call God. They are both so grateful that they were directed to the Church of the Comforter, because now they know that Roscoe is still very much with them.

ANNAMARIA'S STORY

Let parents then bequeath to their children not riches, but the
spirit of reverence
Plato

The death of my mother was a devastating loss. Suddenly, the one who brought me into the world, loved, nurtured, supported, and encouraged me throughout my life, was no longer there. The grief was accompanied by a sense of being orphaned, as I lost my beloved temporary earthly connection to the source of existence. After-death communication reassured me that I was not alone, and that my mother is still very much with me. My spiritual convictions were strengthened through being given the opportunity to connect with the absolute truth: "the soul is immortal and divine."

The ancient historical city of Padova, situated in Northern Italy, is surrounded by the tranquility of the neighboring Euganaean hills and was renowned during the thirteenth and sixteenth centuries as an artistic, scientific, and cultural center. One of its most famous landmarks is the Basilica de San Antonio, where thousands of pilgrims still flock every year to pay homage to the shrine of the saint whose earthly remains are preserved there. The Basilica holds many fabulous art treasures, including eight sculptures by Donatello that adorn the high altar. There is a palpable sacred energy stored in the narrow cobbled streets and historical buildings. These include the university, which was founded in 1222 and attracted many renowned philosophers and teachers, such as Dante and Petrach. Padova was also the setting for Shakespeare's famous play *The Taming of the Shrew*.

* * * * *

Annamaria

Every summer during my childhood, we would leave the small coastal town in England where I grew up, and visit my mother's family in Padova. After crossing the English Channel, I would watch through the train windows as the Simplon or Orient Express would leave Paris. We crossed northern France and wended our way through Switzerland, passing picturesque lakes, mountains and villages. Finally, we'd cross the Italian border. My grandfather would usually come to meet us at the station in Padova, and we would arrive at my grandparent's home tired and dusty from the long journey. We would be welcomed by my mother's large exuberant family, and the delicious aromas that emanated from my grandmother's kitchen.

My grandfather was a book binder, who bound the most beautiful books by hand, and I always remember the earthy smell of parchment and glue that came from the little room he used to work from. It was often a struggle for him to provide enough for the family to survive. But though they were often short of material possessions, the heartfelt welcome and love we received was never in short supply. I am always grateful for my Italian heritage, and the opportunity it provided to become imbued with the important and sacred aspects of life.

As a young woman during the final years of the Second World War, my mother, Vanna, had often been brave and courageous in the efforts to help move stranded Allied soldiers hidden in the local church, down the resistance line and back to safety. She often related stories of her daring exploits and bold adventures.

One day, she told me how she had been with two servicemen, and it had been arranged that a bus driver would stop and pick them up outside of the church. The bus arrived and they set off towards the next rendezvous. A short time later, a German patrol boarded the bus and asked everyone for their papers. When it came to my mother's turn, she showed her papers, and the false ones that had been made up for the two young men she was escorting. Suddenly, one of the German soldiers returned and asked one of these men a question and he couldn't answer, because he couldn't speak the language. My mother said the first thing that came into her head, saying that the two were her brothers and they had both been born deaf and mute. She then recounted how an amazing thing happened for, as she looked directly into the clear blue eyes of the young officer, they seemed to exchange some kind of intense recognition of each other. She knew in an instant that he didn't believe her, but he simply acknowledged her and walked away, saving her life and that of the two men who were with her.

Sometimes, the men wouldn't make it; they would get rounded up on raids carried out in the local churches. My mother told me of how she would follow the German patrols and their captives to the railway station. She would be deeply upset and recite a prayer for them, as she watched them being loaded onto the cattle trucks that would lead them to languish in prisoner-of-war camps, or perish in Nazi Germany. For many years, she would receive Christmas cards from some of the airmen and soldiers who had made it back. They never forgot her, or the enormous personal risk she took to help them.

Later, my mother became a war bride, who met and married my father, an English soldier, stationed in Padova. After their marriage, she moved to England and began a new life. She was a vibrant woman, who soon learned and became fluent in English and settled down to bring up a family. In her spare time, she taught Italian and Italian literature to a large number of students for many years. Vanna loved her home, her children and her grandchildren, and she had a great affinity with nature. The only mar in her world was a virulent form of skin cancer that had probably been originally caused by exposure to the long hot summers of her childhood.

Her illness was a long, tormenting and cruel one. It caused her much anguish and suffering and, for a beautiful woman, it was also debilitating, as operation after operation and treatment after treatment was carried out on her face to try to stop the spread of the disease. None of them worked, and we stood by trying to offer support and comfort as she finally lost an eye to the disease, and later became robbed of her eyesight entirely. Slowly, she lost the ability to do all the things she enjoyed most in life, like taking long walks in the woods and forests, traveling to different places, and above all, being able to see the world around her. She was a great gardener and her garden was her sanctuary, in which she loved to tend her favorite pink roses and feed the many wild birds that made their home in the surroundings.

Her long journey was a torturous one, and gradually it became apparent that she was not going to win the battle, as the skin grafts transplanted to her face showed up to be infected and spread the disease still further. It was a tough test of her faith and, although she never complained, towards the end, she started to give up hope on life, and we knew we were on the downward path. What sense was there to be made of such suffering and pain? My family tried to understand the things we all try to fathom: why would someone who had never done anybody any harm, and who had always extended herself to others, go through so much? At such times it is very difficult to come to terms with such events, and it is often only upon reflection that one is able to glimpse the gift another's suffering brings into fruition.

In our home, the one thing my parents had never been able to talk about was death. This was strange in a way, for when my mother was a child of seven, a terrible epidemic of a childhood disease had swept through Padova, and her childhood friend had fallen ill and later died. On the night of this little girl's death, my mother had awakened to see her friend sitting at the end of the bed, dressed in a shimmering white dress. She was smiling and telling my mother not to worry because she was all right. This after-death communication was so vivid that my mother retained the image and the certainty of the validity of this vision for the rest of her life.

Our entire family had also got used to living with the results of paranormal psychic activities after my father renovated a four-hundred-year-old cottage that we moved into. Independently, we had all experienced the presence of an entity co-habiting with us, although we had never openly discussed the matter with each other. But, one day, while walking in the woods, I blurted out to my father, "Dad, I think there's a ghost in our house." I fully expected him to tell me that I was imagining things, but to my surprise, he simply looked at me, and said, "Oh, so you've felt it too." We all got used to living alongside this abnormal presence, and named her "Dora," because every evening, at around 10:00 p.m., the front door would sound as if it had been opened, and we could hear the click of the lock and the sound of the door closing, followed by footsteps mounting the stairs. This ghostly activity seemed quite harmless and never bothered us, but when we were taking care of a friend's dog, it intuitively picked up the sense of an abnormal presence and went berserk during the night, pulling down the drapes and howling until dawn. The following morning, we had to take the dog to the kennel, until the owners returned.

My parents, like most people, had experienced paranormal happenings that suggested very strongly the possibility of an afterlife or altered realms of reality. While on a troop ship sailing around the Mediterranean, my father had awakened one night to the sound of what he described as being a "heavenly choir." The beautiful music was so compelling that he was drawn to get up and search the entire ship to find the source it emanated from. He could find nothing to explain this eerie phenomenon, and stood leaning over the rail contemplating the moonlit waters below him, until the sound faded away. Years later, he told the story to a friend, and much to his astonishment, she advised him that she had just finished reading a book that described the same kind of happenings.

My father wrote to the author, who had compiled stories of people purporting to share the same experience in the same geographical area. He confirmed that according to his research, in which he had encountered many similar stories, my father had heard the sound of the famous Greek sirens. In Greek mythology, the sirens were known to captivate sailors with their beautiful voices and melodies, and legend has it that they lured many ships to their doom as they sailed into the jagged cliffs and rocks.

But even though my parents had both experienced this type of confirmation of there being something beyond our limited understanding of the mysteries of life, they were not able to expand this knowledge into dealing with the concept of physical death. When my grandfather died, they didn't even tell me immediately. I remember spending the last summer with him. When I left to return to England, I hugged him goodbye; we exchanged a glance and, somehow, I knew that I would never see him again. He kissed me on the cheek, and said, "Ciao, Bella, Ciao," and those were the last words he ever spoke to me. A few months later, I saw my mother sitting at the kitchen table crying, and asked, "What has happened?" She was so overcome with grief that she couldn't speak. I knew then that my grandfather had died. That was my first exposure to the taboo surrounding death. I was sixteen years old and went up to my bedroom and lay on my bed, overwhelmed with sadness.

Several decades later, I was going to have to face going through this painful process of losing a family member again, but I wanted to prepare myself to be with my mother in a far more conscious way, and engage with her fully in the process of her transition. Although I had been born into a Catholic family, and had attended a convent for all of my school years, the concepts the church presented seemed so regimented and full of conditions for an afterlife that I had abandoned my faith when I moved away from home, and I started to look toward Eastern concepts to expand my knowledge and awareness. I believed that there was something more, but it seemed hard to recapture this elusive memory. But life has a tendency to take you to where you are meant to go, and provides the path to spiritual understanding, if only we can be open to these possibilities.

The guiding hand of a higher power led me to a small private University in Ojai, where all the school programs were very much aimed at fostering the belief in conscious living and dying, and the continuum of consciousness after physical death. I glanced through the curriculum; it seemed to offer classes that would indeed expand my knowledge. Even though I had worked in hospice and knew that rather than being a morbid place full of fear, it was in fact the most beautiful and peaceful environment, in which the sanctity of transition from this world to the next was a very profound experience — this knowledge didn't seem to help much in facing my mother's death. The truth was that I was terrified of losing her and of not having that loving connection in my life. The death of a parent is so painful, because we lose our core sense of family, and losing the mother who brought us into the world often makes us feel as though we are orphaned and have lost our source connection.

Gradually, I began to further my knowledge around death and the dying process. Not long after I had enrolled, one of the founders of the school, who had a resolute belief in the afterlife and who had experienced many altered states of consciousness, made her transition. Following the observance of her cultural traditions, her body was laid out in the school chapel during her memorial service. I had never seen an open casket and, to begin with, I thought the whole process very macabre, so I attended the service not knowing what to expect. As I walked passed the coffin and gazed at Dominga's face, I was overcome with a sense of peace. She looked so serene in death; her face looking smooth and almost youthful. I then fully understood the value of such a ritual, for I knew at that moment, without any shadow of doubt that I was looking at an empty shell. It wasn't the traumatic experience that I had expected, because Dominga's essence or spirit had departed to another level of existence, and it was only the earthly body that was left behind. This awareness opened me up to a greater understanding of the reality of the death-and-dying process. As I continued my studies, I became very interested in the near-death experience, and realized how valuable these accounts were in providing evidence for the afterlife.

All this could not have come at a better time, because my mother's condition was deteriorating. I made a decision to be fully consciously present with her, physically whenever possible, but psychically all the time, and to accompany her as far as I could go on her journey to the next world.

This was a deep, sacred and profound experience, with times of joy, deep sadness, incredible insights and interactions with altered states of consciousness. It proved to be a journey of discovery and growth, full of many precious moments. One of the things my mother could no longer do was to take walks with me. All through the years that my children were growing up, this was one of the things we most enjoyed doing together. So, one day, I said to her, "I know you can't physically come with me, but I'm going to take you psychically with me every morning, when I take the dog out, and all you have to do is to try and connect with me." Her face lit up at the idea, so every day that's what I did. I would describe where we were and what we had seen, what the weather was like and all the things of interest that we had encountered along the way. I know this practice gave my mother the opportunity to use her imagination to transcend the fact that she could no longer move around or see well and that it brought her a few moments of happiness each day. Often, I would sit on a rock by a vernal pool, and tell her what a great mother and grand-mother she had been, and that although we would miss her dreadfully, she must feel free when the time came to leave us. All the while, I felt a strong sense of connection with her that I know she shared.

All of her life, my mother had felt very close to the Virgin Mary, and so I always said a Hail Mary for her; it was a prayer that I had not recited for many years, but it served as a very peaceful meditation that I found very comforting. My mother had a great affection for donkeys and mules; they were her favorite charity. In a field I passed each day, there was an old mule. It became part of my routine to stop and give him a carrot or an apple, and I knew how much my mother would have enjoyed seeing him. I grew to love this old mule; there was something so ancient, sturdy and comforting buried in his old bones. Somehow, he had the power to reassure me and one day, when I looked deeply into his liquid brown eyes, they seemed like vast pools that symbolized eternity. For a moment, I felt connected to something so much greater than everyday reality.

Gradually, my mother started to become disorientated, and the treatments she had been undergoing left her weak and frail. She started to detach and separate from this world, which is a stage that a dying person goes through as he or she prepares to make the transition. One day, when I was driving along through a country lane, I felt as if a jolt of lightning had passed through my body. Suddenly, I could see a black and white film running in my mind. I saw my mother and father standing in St. Mark's square in Venice, where they spent their honeymoon. I could feel my mother's excitement at the prospect of her new life in England. I was there in that place and time, even though it was several years before I was born. I knew for certain in that moment that this period of time still existed, and that our whole concept of the past, the present, and the future is just an illusion. It was the strangest feeling, and then suddenly everything returned to normal.

A short while after I had returned home, my son, Jay, called to tell me that he had been to see my mother and that she was no longer speaking in English, but appeared to be rambling in Italian, and that he couldn't understand her. But I knew where she was, because I had been there with her. My son then started to leave, thinking that my mother didn't know that he was there, but just as he turned the door handle, she spoke in a very lucid and clear voice, saying in English, "Pray for me now."

Visitors from other realms started to make their presence felt around my mother in the six weeks prior to her death. One morning, she woke up very excited and animated, and wanted to tell me about the people who had come to her the night before; she recognized them as being departed family members, although some of them she didn't know, and she said, "They were all urging me to leave with them, because they are going to take me to a wonderful place that has the most beautiful garden." The visitors continued to appear at night, and my mother remained happily excited when she recounted their visits. One morning, I said to her, "You are free to go with them whenever you feel you want to." She replied, saying, "No. I'm not quite ready yet."

Sometimes, Vanna would appear to be talking to her father who seemed to be very close by, and she would get agitated and upset when his presence seemed to leave for a while. My family tended to believe that she was just suffering from delusions or dementia, and brushed off these interactions, but I knew of many cases of end-of-life or deathbed visions, and rather than patronize her, I would encourage her to describe these comforting experiences.

My mother and I had become far closer after my children were born; she loved being a grandmother, and showered both of her grandchildren with unconditional love. Although I knew that she loved me, she had never really told me so verbally. One day, when the house was full of people visiting, she suddenly sat up and was looking at me as she beckoned to the others in the room. She said, "Can you see her? This is my beautiful daughter, she's so beautiful and she was beautiful from the day she was born." She seemed so excited to relate this message, and repeated it several times. I was overcome; it was a validation that I had needed from her all of my life. It appeared to be a benediction or a blessing that came through her, and it is something I treasure and will never forget, for it cemented our relationship for eternity.

Shortly after, we celebrated my mother's seventy-seventh birthday. She had slipped further away and I wasn't sure that she recognized us any more, but my son and I wheeled her into the garden, as it was such a beautiful day. As we stood there for a moment, I tried to think of a way to connect with her, and so I asked her if she remembered sitting out in the garden with the children when they were young and singing to them. I wasn't sure if she had understood me, so I started to sing one of her favorite songs. After a few bars, and much to our delight, she joined in and started to sing along, even though she hadn't spoken any English for several weeks. It was the last interaction we had in a conscious state.

I was at the time commuting between England and the United States, and shortly after Vanna's birthday, I returned to New York for my younger son's graduation from drama school. I had only been back for two weeks, when the phone call came. It was my father, and he said, "Mum's been suffering a lot of pain and has been put on a morphine drip, and it's now only a question of time." I immediately booked a flight, but couldn't get out until the next day, so I called my father back, and said, "Tell mum to wait for me." And he replied, "She's not conscious and won't under-stand." And I said, "Just be sure to tell her." He said that he would do so.

Before leaving, I called my friend, Reuben Beckham, who assured me everything would be all right. He gave me strength, and reminded me to tell my mother that there was no reason to be afraid — that she would not be alone and that her journey would take her back home. Reuben has a very definite connection to the spirit world, and I took his meaning to be that if I could let go of my fears and all the things I had to take care of, I would get back in touch with the connection he embodies. I then walked to the vernal pool with my dearest friend, Gael, who had been so supportive through my many months of anguish. We did a little ceremony, and made a little boat from some large leaves, filling it with vibrant yellow blossom. We placed this cocoon in the water and said a prayer for Vanna's safe transition. I told my mother that I was on my way, and asked her again to wait for me if she could, because I wanted to be with her.

When I arrived at my home in England, I paused to collect the things that I knew would offer my mother comfort, a bunch of pink roses from her garden, a candle of the Virgin of Guadalupe, and a picture of my younger son, Toby, who was still in the States. I then went straight to the hospital and saw this tiny frail figure still valiantly fighting for each labored breath, and I knew that it would not be long before she left us.

We gathered around my mother's bedside, my brother, son and I; my father was too overcome and couldn't face the vigil, but as the evening wore on and it became dark, a peaceful presence entered the room. We sat together stroking Vanna's arms and holding her hands, and we talked to her and about her as we sat drinking some red wine. We reminisced about the past, and all the things we remembered and had shared together. We were in a deep sacred space where time and the outside world had no meaning, and then the nurse came in and told us that it was safe to leave for a while and get a bit of rest.

In the early morning, I sat in my mother's beloved garden and collected myself for the final moments. Later that afternoon, after sitting with her, my brother left for a short while to attend to some business matters, and my son needed to get a breath of fresh air. I was alone with my mother, and I told her once more how much we all loved her, and that she had been a wonderful wife, mother and grandmother, and that it was now okay for her to leave, even though we would miss her. Two minutes later, she took her final breath and passed away peacefully. She died on the twenty-first of May, traditionally known in the Roman Catholic faith as the month honoring the Virgin Mary. My two children were born in this month, and my mother made her transition on the day that fell exactly between their two birthdays.

My brother returned a moment later and, although he does not have strong religious convictions, he decided to open the window, just in case her soul should exit through it. My son came back and said his final goodbye. I went outside into the fresh, cool evening air and above my head, a flock of swallows suddenly appeared, soaring majestically into the sky. I believe my mother's soul was with them.

That night, I lay fitfully dozing and I awoke fully around 4:00 a.m. In the room that I was sleeping in, my mother had placed a head-and-shoulders porcelain image of the Virgin Mary holding the baby Jesus in her arms, with her face turned to the side. This icon had always been there, as long as I remember. As I looked over to the wall, a glowing light filled the area where the image was hanging. Slowly, the light expanded to fill up most of the room, as the features of Mary slowly turned into the features of my mother's face. I stared at it for quite a while, and then the light began to fade and the image reverted back to normal. I knew this was a sign of my mother's presence, because she had always felt close to

Mary, and it had also become part of my practice to say the Hail Mary every day. In fact on reflection, I realized that it was an obvious way for her to make her presence known, for being a loving mother and grandmother had been the most important parts of Vanna's life.

As with all deaths, the next few days were spent in a numbing sort of grief, and busily filled with all the arrangements that needed to be made. My father wanted to get everything over with as soon as possible, and wanted a quick cremation, but I knew it wouldn't have been what my mother would have wanted. In the end, we decided to have a service in the local village church. On the day of her funeral, we walked through the village that had been her home for so many years and to the church, following her coffin that was covered in pink roses. Many friends had gathered to pay tribute, and we celebrated her life while listening to the beautiful music of Andrea Boceli, one of her favorite singers that she had enjoyed greatly, in the last few months of her life.

I had written a eulogy for my mother, but knew that I couldn't face reading it, so I asked my younger son who, as an actor, I thought would manage to read it well. He started off confidently enough, but after the first few lines, he began to falter and then broke down into floods of the deepest grief. The minister looked at me and intimated that perhaps I might like to intervene, but I decided not to. I knew that Toby was expressing the overwhelming grief for everyone, and it needed to be felt and expressed, for we had lost the physical presence of a precious person in our lives, and things would never be the same without her.

It took a lot of courage for him to stand there in front of so many people, with tears streaming down his face, but Toby took a deep breath and eventually carried on, adding some of his own words, saying, "I could be in the darkest place and feeling really bad about myself but, in Nan's eyes, I always shone in the brightest light, and that was her gift of unconditional love that I have been fortunate enough to experience all my life."

As we filed out of the church at the end of the service to the beautiful sound of *Ave Maria* filling the small church, I felt as though my mother was very close by. That evening, when walking up the stairs of my parents home, I could smell her perfume. It was just in one small area of the landing, but it was unmistakable, and a further sign of her continuing presence.

Shortly after the funeral, I went to Italy with my brother and children, and we visited my mother's sisters and family members, who were all deeply upset at the loss. While visiting Chioggia, we went into one of the open churches. I wanted to light candle for my mother, but all of the altars were closed. We walked around and met a caretaker, who said he would open one of the altars. Out of the many small chapels honoring the many saints, he happened to choose one that was designated to Mary, and said we could light all the candles that were formed in the shape of a heart, entwined in a bed of pink roses. In that cool sacred space, we were with my mother in her homeland, and she was with us.

A short time later, I had the most vivid dream of Vanna. It was the sort of dream that many people experience after the death of a loved one, in the form of an after-death communication. In the dream, I got out of bed and in front of me stood my mother. She was so close that I could almost feel the woolen hairs on the jacket she had on. It was a jacket that she had worn a lot in the last few months of her life. Instinctively, I knew that if I took my eyes off her that she would vanish but, at the same time, I wanted to call to my son who was in the next room and tell him to come quickly.

Feverishly, I fixed my concentration on my mother and simultaneously, I called my son's name. I followed her towards a door, and then she turned and held her hand up saying that I could come no further. She was crying and I wanted to reach out and touch her. I was upset because she still looked as frail as she had before she died but, she pointed to another room that had an open door and, as I looked inside the room, I saw her lying on a bed. She was young and beautiful, smiling and wearing a pretty summer dress, with a look of deep contentment on her face. Suddenly, I understood her message. It had all been so painful at the end, and the images I retained were of someone struggling and suffering. I knew that in that moment, she wanted me to see her transformation and not remember her as she was in her final days, but as she is now.

I experienced many further strange happenings, which I could have put down to coincidence, but for the fact that they were all so pertinently and subtly connected to my mother. Vanna loved jewelry and had many fine pieces. Sometimes, I would admire one that she was wearing, and she would laughingly say, "One day it will be yours." Following her death, my father gave me some of her bracelets and necklaces, which I often wear. On numerous occasions, I would be sitting typing this manuscript, when suddenly; a bracelet or necklace of hers that I had on would come undone and drop on to the desk in front of me. I did take a couple of the bracelets in for repair, thinking that the clasp must have come loose, but I was assured that they were fine and that there was no reason for them to be replaced. I came to believe that these occurrences were signs that my mother was encouraging me in the work I was doing.

My mother's death was a deep and profound journey, and it changed my life forever. There is no easy way to say goodbye, and no escape from grief, which has its own timetable. The dying process of a loved one brings times of great sadness and mourning, and also moments of great beauty and clarity that connect us to a higher state of consciousness. Everyone in the family had to face many challenges, but grief opened our hearts and enabled an inner strength to emerge in each of us.

Through my mother's suffering, we all gained a greater awareness of ourselves and the meaning of relationships, and how important it is to tell the people you love how much you care about them. For my older son, the experience brought the best out in him as a human being for, as a young man who had no experience in dealing with such a painful situation, he made the decision to return to England for the final six months of his grandmother's life. It made such a difference to her to have him around. He took her to doctor's appointments, made her laugh, and loved her in such a sensitive and courageous way that reflected the deep commitment and connection they shared, in a manner that was far beyond his years. My younger son, who had a troubled and difficult childhood, was able to express all the grief he had experienced for most of his life and, at Vanna's funeral, he grieved for all the places he needed to be free from. His deepest regret is that his beloved grandmother wasn't physically here to share his hard-earned success when his first movie was released a couple of years later.

My mother gave me the greatest of gifts, for her death made me look at my own life and make long-needed changes. I came to understand that her suffering and pain were not in vain, for she touched us all through her courageous battle and, as a result, I think she made us better human beings.

* * * * *

Following my after-death communications with my mother, I became more fully convinced in life after death, and realized how many people are afraid of facing their own and other's mortality, because they believe that it is the end. Through my experiences, I have learned that fully embracing death does help us to understand the great mysteries of existence: why we are here, why we suffer, and where we go when we die. My mother's courageous struggle with a long and cruel illness robbed her of her mobility and her sight, but it never claimed her spirit. Although she suffered greatly, until the end, she remained, a woman *full of grace*, who taught me so much. And I often contemplated and found comfort in the words of the poet T. S. Eliot, who said:

And the time of death is every moment
Which shall fructify in the lives of others

I decided to do something altruistic with my experience, and something that I believe my mother would be proud of. I consulted a psychic shortly after her death, who told me I was going to write a book of modern-day parables that would help people come to terms with the dying process and appreciate the preciousness and beauty of life. This is the result of my endeavors, with the help of all the people who have offered their contributions, encouragement and support to my efforts. It is my sincerest wish that those who read this will find these stories to be inspirational and spiritually uplifting, and that they will help them to become fully engaged in the process of conscious living and dying — knowing that one day, they too, will leave earthly existence and merge into the loving presence of a continuum of consciousness.

BIBLIOGRAPHY

Alighieri, Dante. *The Divine Comedy* (translated by Allen Mandelbaum). USA: Everyman's Library, 1955.

Andrews, Tamara. *A Dictionary of Nature Myths.* New York: Oxford University Press, 1998.

Bede, Venerables. *A History of the English Church and People.* UK: Penguin Classics, 1955.

Campbell, Joseph. *The Hero with a Thousand Faces.* New York: Princeton/Bollingen, 1968.

Dossey, Larry. *Prayer is Good Medicine.* San Francisco: Harper Collins, 1996.

Eliade, Mircea. *Shamanism: Archaic States of Ecstasy.* (translated by.Willard R. Trask), USA: Princeton/Bollingen, 1964.

Easwaran, Eknath (translator). *The Bhagavad Gita.* USA: The Blue Mountain Center of Meditation, 1985.

Evans-Wentz, W.Y. *Tibetan Yoga and Sacred Doctrines.* New York: Oxford University Press, 1973.

Frankl, Viktor. *Man's Search for Meaning.* New York: Pocket Books, 1963.

Freemantle, Francesca (translated by Chogyam Trungpa). *The Tibetan Book of the Dead.* Boston: Shambhala, 2000.

Gallup, George Jr. *Adventures in Immortality.* USA: McGrawHill, 1982.

Greeley, Andrew. *Death and Beyond.* Chicago: Thomas More Association, 1976.

Hagman, Larry. *Hello Darlin'.* New York: Simon & Schuster, 2001.

Hillman, James. *Re-Visioning Psychology.* New York: Harper Perrenial, 1976.

Jung, C.G. *Memories, Dreams Reflections.* (edited by Aniela Jaffe, translated by Richard and Clara Winston). New York: Vintage Books, 1989.

Jung, C.G. *The Earth Has a Soul* (edited by Meredith Sabini). California: North Atlantic Books, 2002

Kubler-Ross, Elisabeth. *A Memoir of Living and Dying*. New York: Touchstone, 1998.

Levine, Stephen. *A Year to Live*. USA: Harmony/Bell Tower, 1998.

Luke, Helen M. *Dark Wood to White Rose*. New Mexico: Dove Publications, 1972.

Martin, Joel and Patricia Romanowski. *Love Beyond Life*. New York: Harper Collins, 1997.

Moody, Raymond, and Elisabeth Kubler-Ross. *Life after Life*. USA: Harper Collins, 2001.

Moody, Raymond. *Reunions*. New York: Ballantine Books, 1993.

Nasr. Seyyed Hossein (editor). *Islamic Spirituality*. New York: Crossroads, 1987.

Neihardt, John G. *Black Elk Speaks*. USA: Pocket Books, 1972.

Osis, Karlis. *Deathbed Observations of Physicians and Nurses* USA: Parapsychology Foundation, 1961.

Patel, Krit. Vijay, C. Amin. *Yoga of Action: Compilation from Divine Teachings of Bhagavan Sri Sathya Sai Baba*. India: Patel & Vijay, date unknown.

Plato. *Republic* (translated by F.M. Cornford). USA: Oxford University Press, 1951.

Plato. *Republic* (translated by G.M.A. Grube). Indianapolis: Hackett Publishing, 1992.

Rilke, Ranier Maria. *Sonnets to Orpheus* (translated by M. D. Herter). Norton, New York: W. W. Norton & Company, 1992.

Ring, Kenneth. *Lessons from the Light*. New Hampshire: Monument Point Press, 2000.

Ring, Kenneth. *Life at Death*. USA: William Morrow & Co., 1982.

Sabom, Michael. *Light and Death*. Michigan: Zondervan, 1998.

Shroder, Thomas. *Old Souls: Compelling Evidence from Children who remember Past Lives*. New York: Fireside, 2001.

Stevenson, Ian. *Twenty Cases Suggestive of Reincarnation.* USA: Virginia University Press, 1980.

Other Sources

Thich Nhat Hahn. *A Public Talk at the Riverside Church.* New York; www.theconversation.org/essence.html. May, 2006.

Chopra, Swati. *Ancient Wisdom, Modern Mind.* www.lifepositive.com/Spirit/world-Religions/Buddhism/dalailama.asp. May, 2006.

Fenwick, Peter. *Spring Journal,* 2005. www.iands.org. May, 06.

Fenwick, Peter. *American Journal of Hospice and Palliative Medicine,* 2006.

Works Cited

The Near-Death Experience – Not the end, but a new beginning

1. Plato. *Republic.* (Tr. F. M. Cornford. USA: Oxford University Press, 1951), p. 355.

2. Eliade, Mircea. *Shamanism: Archaic States of Ecstasy.* (Tr. Willard R. Trask. USA: Princeton/Bollingen, 1964), p. 393.

3. Eliade, Mircea. *Shamanism: Archaic States of Ecstasy.* (Tr. Willard R. Trask. USA: Princeton/Bollingen), 1964), p. 394.

4. Fenwick, Peter. *Journal of Near-Death Studies.* (Spring, 2005. www.iands.org).

5. Sabom, Michael. *Light and Death.* (Michigan: Zondervan, 1998), p.p. 12-16.

6. Plato. *Republic.* (Tr. G. M. A. Grube. Indianapolis: Hackett Publishing, 1992), p. 290.

7. Luke, Helen M. *Dark Wood to White Rose.* (New Mexico: Dove Publications, 1972), p. 4.

8. Campbell, Joseph. *The Hero with a Thousand Faces.* (New York: Princeton/Bollingen, 1968), p. 16.

9. Edman, Irwin. *The Philosophy of Plato.* (New York: The Modern

Library, 1928), p.122.

Dying to Experience Life

1. Plato. *Republic*. (Tr. G. M. A. Grube. Indianapolis: Hackett Publishing, 1992), p. 292.

2. Rilke, Rainer Maria. *Sonnets to Orpheus*. (Tr. M. D. Herter Norton. New York: W. W. Norton & Company, 1992), p. 132).

3. Patel, Krit. Vijay, C. Amin. *Yoga of Action: Compliation from Divine Teachings of Bhagavan Sathya Sai Baba*. (India: Patel & Vijay: unknown publishing date), p. 61.

4. Chopra, Swati. *Ancient Wisdom, Modern Mind*. www.lifepositive.com/Spirit/world-Religions/Buddhism/dalailama.asp. May, 06

5. Thich Nhat Hahn. *A Public Talk at the Riverside Church*. New York. www.theconversation.org/essence.html. May, 06.

6. Patel, Krit. Vijay, C. Amin. *Yoga of Action: Compilation of Action:Compliation from Divine Teachings of Bhagavan Sri Sathya Sai Baba*. (India: Patel & Vijay: unknown publishing date), p. 9.

7. Frankl, Viktor. Man's Search for Meaning. (New York: Pocket Books, 1963), p. p. 103-104.

Birth, death and rebirth: A continuum of Consciousness

1. Frankl, Viktor. Man's Search for Meaning. (New York: Pocket Books, 1963), p.p. 109-110.

2. Andrews, Tamara. *A Dictionary of Nature Myths*. (New York: Oxford University Press, 1988), p. 53.

3. Jung, C.G. *The Earth has a Soul*. (Ed. Meredith Sabini. California: North Atlantic Books, 2002), p. 97.

4. Jung, C.G. *The Earth has a Soul*. (Ed. Meredith Sabini. California: North Atlantic Books. 2002), p. 59.

5. Eliade, Mircea. *Shamansim: Archaic States of Ecstasy*. (Tr. Willard R. Trask. USA: Princeton/Bollingen, 1964), p. 460.

6. Eliade, Mircea. *Shamanism: Arcahic States of Ecstasy*. (Tr. Willard R Trask. USA: Princton/Bollingen, 1964), p.p. 408-409.

7. Frankl, Viktor. *Man's Search for Meaning* (New York: Pocket Books, 1963), p.64.

8. Evans-Wentz. W. Y. *Tibetan Yoga and Secret Doctrines*. (New York: Oxford University Press, 1973), p.p. 253-254.

9. Freemantle, Francesca. Tr., Chogyam Trungpa. *The Tibetan Book of the Dead*. (Boston: Shambhala, 2000), p.p. 2-3.

10. Hillman, James. *Re-Visioning Psychology*. (New York: Harper Perrenial, 1976), p.110.

11. Martin, Joel, and Patricia Romanowski. *Love Beyond Life*. New York: HarperCollins, 1997), p. xxii.

12. Dossey, Larry, *Prayer is good Medicine*. (San Francisco: HarperCollins, 1996), p. 156.

13. Edman, Irwin., Ed. *The Philosophy of Plato*. (New York: The Modern Library, New York, 1928), p. 188.